Traveller from Tokyo

Written with a most charming and self effacing style, this book offers readers a fascinating insight into Japan and Japanese life at the eve of its fateful entry into the Second World War.

The author, who had spent much time in India and had written on the Sikim Himalayas, was engaged by the Japanese government as an advisor to the Japanese Foreign Office in Tokyo and as a lecturer in Tokyo.

www.keganpaul.com

THE KEGAN PAUL
JAPAN LIBRARY

The National Faith of Japan • *D.C. Holtom*
The Japanese Enthronement Ceremonies • *D.C. Holtom*
History of Japanese Religion • *Masaharu Anesaki*
Ainu Creed and Cult • *Neil Gordon Munro*
Japan: Its Architecture, Art and Art Manufactures • *Christopher Dresser*
An Artist's Letters from Japan • *John La Farge*
Japanese Girls and Women • *Alice M. Bacon*
The Kwaidan of the Lady of Tamiya • *James S. de Benneville*
The Haunted House • *James S. de Benneville*
We Japanese • *Frederic de Garis and Atsuharu Sakai*
Shogi: Japanese Chess • *Cho-Yo*
The Nightless City of the Geisha • *J. E. de Becker*
Landscape Gardening in Japan • *Josiah Conder*
Things Japanese • *Basil Hall Chamberlain*
The Gardens of Japan • *Jiro Harada*
Ancient Japanese Rituals and the Revival of Pure Shinto • *Sir Ernest Satow*
with Karl Florenz
History of Japanese Thought • *Hajime Nakamura*
The Mikado's Empire • *W. E. Griffis*
Quaint Customs and Manners of Japan • *Mock Joya*
Beauty in Japan • *Samuel W. Wainwright*
Behind the Japanese Mask • *Robert Craigie*
Human Bullets • *Tadayoshi Sakurai*
In the Bamboo Lands of Japan • *Katharine Schuyler Baxter*
Japan and Its Art • *Marcus B. Huish*
Japanese Marks and Seals • *James Lord Bowes*
Learning the Sacred Way of the Emperor • *Yutaka Hibino*
The Flowers and Gardens of Japan • *Ella Du Cane*
The Last Genro • *Omura Bunji*
The Theory of Japanese Flower Arrangements • *Josiah Conder*
Traveller from Tokyo • *John Morris*

Traveller from Tokyo

My Life in Japan, October 1939 to December 1941

———

John Morris

KEGAN PAUL
London • New York • Bahrain

First published in 2004 by
Kegan Paul Limited
UK: P.O. Box 256, London WC1B 3SW, England
Tel: 020 7580 5511 Fax: 020 7436 0899
E-Mail: books@keganpaul.com
Internet: http://www.keganpaul.com
USA: 61 West 62nd Street, New York, NY 10023
Tel: (212) 459 0600 Fax: (212) 459 3678
Internet: http://www.columbia.edu/cu/cup

Distributed by:
Turpin Distribution
Blackhorse Road
Letchworth, Herts. SG6 1HN
England
Tel: (01462) 672555 Fax: (01462) 480947
Email: books@turpinltd.com

Columbia University Press
61 West 62nd Street, New York, NY 10023
Tel: (212) 459 0600 Fax: (212) 459 3678
Internet: http://www.columbia.edu/cu/cup

© Kegan Paul, 2004

Printed in the USA by IBT/Biddles

All Rights reserved. No part of this book may be reprinted or
reproduced or utilised in any form or by any electric, mechanical
or other means, now known or hereafter invented, including
photocopying or recording, or in any information storage or retrieval
system, without permission in writing from the publishers.

ISBN: 0-7103-0886-8

British Library Cataloguing in Publication Data
Morris, John
Traveller from Tokyo : my life in Japan, October 1939 to December 1941. – New ed. –
(The Kegan Paul Japan library)
1.Morris, John – Homes and haunts – Japan 2.British – Japan 3.Japan – Social life and customs – 1912-1945 4.Japan – Description and travel
I.Title
953'.033'092

Library of Congress Cataloging-in-Publication Data
Applied for.

CONTENTS

1937   *Prologue*   1

MY LIFE IN JAPAN (October 1938 to December 1941)

1	How I went to Japan	6
2	Arrival in Yokohama	7
3	The Imperial Hotel, Tokyo	8
4	Finding a house	9
5	Concerning the telephone	13
6	Engaging a servant	15
7	Japanese food	18
8	Japanese dress	22
9	The Japanese language	26
10	Education	33
11	The Japanese mentality	42
12	The English language in Japan	46
13	The Japanese Press	49
14	Literature in Japan	53
15	Mountaineering	57
16	Games and sports	62
17	Marriage	64
18	Geisha and prostitution	69
19	The stage and cinema	72
20	Radio broadcasting	81
21	Western music in Japan	84
22	The changing times	88

AFTER PEARL HARBOUR (7th December 1941 to 29th July 1942)

1	The outbreak of war	91
2	Japanese police methods	95
3	Japanese criminal procedure	101
4	Personal story	107
5	Rationing	108
6	Air Raid Precautions: the American air raid	113
7	My Japanese friends	117
8	Austerity measures: the ban on amusements; changes in education	120
9	Personal story	127
10	The Japanese army	131
11	Personal story	138
12	Departure from Japan	139
★	Postscript	145

PROLOGUE 1937

I WAS THE ONLY PASSENGER WAITING TO BOARD THE PLANE AT CALcutta. It was on its way across India to the Dutch East Indies. Pools of water lay all over the aerodrome, parts of which were covered with a rank growth of weeds and grass, and there was some doubt whether the plane would be able to land. The noon-day heat was almost visible; it seemed to be bubbling up out of the ground, forming small mirages, so that one could hardly tell which was real water, which imaginary.

The hot damp affected everyone and everything. Beads of moisture trickled down the walls of the concrete waiting shed, trickled down the face of the somnolent Eurasian in charge. He regarded me sleepily, without interest, as I stood on the scales, a typewriter in one hand, a suitcase in the other. Outside, a few coolies, naked except for a loin-cloth, were slowly trundling a large filling-tank, the hose of which trailed along the ground behind them. It would have lightened their work if they had wound it on to its rollers; but either this had not occurred to them, or the effort was too much trouble. They dragged the tank to the edge of the half-obscured landing marks, abandoned it and sat down to smoke. Apparently they could not read the two words of simple English that stared at them, in scarlet letters a foot high, from the side of the tank: " Smoking Prohibited."

There was no one else in sight; the whole place was as deserted as the dead Moghul cities of the north. But to me the scene was typical of my state of mind; I had reached a stage when I could see only the apathy, the deadly inefficiency, like a blight, which in time seems to affect everyone and everything in India.

I supposed I was glad to be leaving; and yet there were some regrets. It could hardly be otherwise after one had lived in a country for fifteen years. But I had lost my curiosity; and when that happens to the Englishman in India it is time for him to leave. No further experience is of any value; its only effect is to blunt the sensibility. Sooner or later there comes a time when one must accept either the standards of one's own people or those of the Indian; drift into a narrow social rut or become a native of the country. Attempts at compromise are not only intellectually dishonest, they lead to a sentimental attitude which is fatal. One begins finding

PROLOGUE

excuses, condoning everybody and everything. So I was on my way to England, via Japan and the United States.

As for me, I had wanted to meet the Indian on equal terms, but I found that long years of servility and a lack of educational facilities make any sort of equal intercourse impossible; and the ramifications of caste, which it seemed we had even strengthened for our own ends, form a gulf that nothing can bridge. The only thing now left was pity; and pity alone is a poor excuse for staying in a country.

And yet undeniably there is much that is seductive about the European's life in India; the host of willing servants, ponies to ride, a large salary and very often little work. It is pleasant, too, to be treated as though one is the salt of the earth. The trouble with most people was that after a short time in the country they accepted their status without question. It is indeed difficult to refuse the greatness that is thrust upon one, especially as one becomes older, but it is vital to do so if one is to remain a civilized being. I had a feeling that I was being pulled with the force of a magnet back into the British fold. I also knew that before this happened it was imperative to escape. That was why I had decided to leave at three days' notice, and to leave by air. I wanted to put as many miles between India and myself as quickly as possible.

The huge Douglas was coming in on time. The low-lying clouds had deadened the sound of its engines, so that it seemed to appear suddenly out of nowhere. It circled twice and then landed, bumping and splashing through the puddles. Ten minutes later it was in the air again, and there below us were the drab miles of India racing by. I had resisted the pull of the magnet; its power lessened with every minute. Looking down on the widening map I seemed to see the events of the past fifteen years unfolding beneath me, in the way that a drowning man is said to see his past. Only this was no death. Rather was it an escape from death in life, and any regrets were stifled by relief and the beauty of the scene that was unfolding beneath me.

We were coming out over the Bay of Bengal, an infinity of opal, calm and translucent, its surface broken here and there by an irregular ring of coruscating whiteness, waves breaking against submerged atolls. Far to the left was a golden smear, the sandy shore of Akyab. The ocean seemed completely empty. All that long afternoon we droned on over it, and never the sight of a ship. Towards evening we met the first low hills of Burma, arid and monotonous, but their very drabness was restful after so many coloured miles. And then they too were passed and there below us, standing up in the lush Irrawaddy plain was the Shwe Dagon Pagoda, looking like a giant phallus; a phallus tricked out with diamonds, for just as we circled

PROLOGUE

to make a landing beyond the city its lights were suddenly switched on.

We left Rangoon in darkness, tearing into the night through a lane of smoking flares. Only the harbour lights were visible, like a constellation fallen to the earth. Presently we turned and headed eastwards. We were flying through a void of blackness, but soon a greenish purple glow suffused our private world. It turned to a cold metallic blue, faded and left us again in darkness; then a minute later the sun was gilding our silver wing tips. We turned away from it into the south. Suspended above the northern horizon was a line of ice green mountains, their topmost peaks just catching the dawn's first rays. I supposed them to be on the Tibetan border. They looked completely unreal, as though cut out of a strip of metal, giving the impression that there was nothing behind them.

We were losing height rapidly now and it was possible to see the details of what was below. The whole country was as flat as a pancake and most of it appeared to be under water. Here and there were diminutive houses and patches of grassland. They looked at first like bits of green and dark brown velvet floating in an immense bowl of water, but as we came down even lower they resolved themselves into a chequerboard of ricefields. We seemed now to be only a few feet above the earth, but I could see no sign of a landing ground. We banked steeply and suddenly turned, and for one panic-stricken moment I thought we were about to crash. I am not normally superstitious, but I had been expecting this. I had in fact been so certain that I should not survive this flight that before leaving Calcutta I had insured my life. As I now closed my eyes and gripped the arms of my chair it suddenly occurred to me that the certificates, which I meant to have posted, were still in my pocket and would therefore be destroyed with me. A second later we were taxi-ing on to the concrete runway; we had arrived in Bangkok exactly on time.

I had decided to break my journey here and continue overland to French Indo-China. Bangkok is a city that should be looked at only at dusk or dawn. At such times there is a certain attraction about its baroque skyline. In the harsh light of day it is uniformly ugly, a compound of reed-thatched hovels, office buildings and immense sprawling temples. Most of the latter, originally wooden, have been rebuilt in concrete, in the surface of which millions of tiny fragments of coloured glass have been embedded. Their designers seem to have been imbued with only one idea; to avoid a plain surface at all costs. Decoration is plastered on wherever it is possible to stick it, and tinkling ornaments are suspended from every

PROLOGUE

eave and corner. Looking at these temples from close at hand one is dazzled by the multitudinous squiggles and projections, and the general shape of the building escapes one. Indeed, they give the effect that the ornaments were designed first, the actual building being merely a medium on which to display them. The architect, one thinks, must have been inspired by the sight of an overloaded Christmas tree, fantastically decorated with immense prawns and whiskered lobsters. It was a relief to visit the Siamese white elephants and rest one's eyes on their vast undecorated buttocks; a relief and something of a disappointment, for they are not white but pink.

And then on to Saigon and Hong Kong, where I was to take ship for Kobe. The Sino-Japanese war had now been going on for more than a year, and I had been repeatedly told that this was not a suitable time to visit Japan; that it was no longer possible to travel about in the country, and that the people had become hostile to foreigners. I had disregarded these warnings (which turned out to have nothing to justify them), because I did not think that I should ever again visit the East, and before settling down to become a European I wanted to see as much of it as possible.

I spent on this first occasion exactly three weeks in Japan, during which I visited all the scheduled tourist attractions, did all the things that tourists usually do. I was treated with kindness and courtesy everywhere; in spite of the war, the country seemed to a superficial observer to be functioning quite normally. This was in the autumn of 1937. I have always had a childlike passion for sightseeing, but for some reason or other I went through Japan with eyes that did not stare. It seems absurd, but I can only say that from the moment I stepped off the boat in Kobe I had a strange and inexplicable feeling that I had seen all this before. This feeling remained with me, in fact it became stronger wherever I went. And with it went the certain belief that I should visit all these scenes again.

Here is a possible explanation. I had spent my last six months in India in a lonely Himalayan village, high up near the Tibetan border, where I had gone to study the social life of the people. With me I had only one book, Arthur Waley's *The Tale of Genji*, which is a translation of an immensely long Japanese novel written by a Court lady in the tenth century. This book is a classic, which the Japanese hold in great esteem; but by no stretch of imagination can it, in its original form, be described as popular reading. Waley's translation had become, however, a best-seller both in England and America, and it has certainly done more than anything else to make Western readers familiar with ancient Japanese culture. It has been criticised by certain Japanese pedants on the grounds that it is not altogether

PROLOGUE

textually faithful to the original. On this point I am not competent to speak, since I have only the most elementary knowledge of written Japanese. But the matter is unimportant, since from a literary point of view Dr. Waley has produced something that will continue to give pleasure so long as the English language remains. But all this is by the way. The point is that I had so steeped my mind in this book before going to Japan that it may account for the feeling of familiarity that I everywhere had.

While I was in Tokyo I was asked to speak to several of the University Mountaineering clubs on the work of the Mount Everest Expeditions, in two of which I had participated as a sort of general factotum, interpreter and transport officer. I was not, never have been, and have not the necessary physique and agility ever to become, even a moderately good climber; but I have always been fond of mountain travel and have spent a great deal of my leisure in various kinds of mountain exploration. Modern expeditions are elaborate affairs, the administration of which is complicated and often delicate, and my own inclusion in the parties was due solely to a knowledge of local conditions and people. I have to mention this because I found myself described in the local press as " world-famous mountaineer," and nothing I could say succeeded in disillusioning the Japanese public. (My undeserved reputation preceded me to America, where I found myself described in the California papers as " MAN FROM LOST HORIZON.")

Although I had a strong presentiment that I should eventually return, when we sailed from Yokohama on the first day of December it did not seem likely that this would happen. But as a result of giving a few lectures in Tokyo, I came into contact with a number of those engaged in University teaching, and was asked vaguely if I would not like to return and join one or other of the faculties. Nothing definite was offered, however, and I gave no thought to the subject. As a matter of fact I would not at that time have accepted an appointment in Japan. I liked the country and had spent an exceedingly pleasant three weeks in it; but I was now possessed by an overwhelming nostalgia for London. A book of mine had just been accepted and I wanted to stay in England and go on writing.

MY LIFE IN JAPAN
October 1938 to December 1941
★ *1* ★

IT WAS IN THE EARLY SUMMER OF 1938 THAT I FOUND ONE MORNING among my letters an invitation to a reception at the Japanese Embassy. I was beginning to settle down in London and had almost forgotten the tentative suggestions I had received the year before about going back to Japan. I was now to learn that they meant more than I supposed.

There was nothing unusual about the reception; and I was wondering how soon I could decently escape, when one of the Ambassador's secretaries approached me and said that His Excellency would like to see me in his study. He told me that he had received a cable requesting him to offer me a post as adviser to the Japanese Foreign Office, with which was coupled a lectureship in English at one of the Tokyo Universities. I was a little taken aback; the idea of advising a foreign government seemed rather alarming, and I am not given to tendering advice in any circumstances. But it soon came out that I should not be responsible for anything much more important than dotting an occasional *i* and crossing an occasional *t* in the various documents and statements which Tokyo issued in English. "The post," His Excellency said, "is what is called in your language a sinecule." For a moment I stared, then gave a smile. I had forgotten that the Japanese (as also the Chinese), unless they have been educated abroad, often cannot distinguish between the letters *L* and *R*. When his meaning dawned upon me, however, I thought that I was fully qualified to deal with any sinecure; and as for the lectureship, why not? Emboldened by the Embassy champagne, I accepted on the spot. "But first," I said, before leaving the room, "don't you wish to make some further enquiries about me?" wondering to whom I could refer him. "That has already been done," he replied, "we have, moreover, engaged your passage. It will save you trouble."

I had always known that the Japanese were efficient, but I was

ARRIVAL IN YOKOHAMA

surprised. It did not occur to me at the time that I was already experiencing in England a first taste of peculiar police methods, with which I was to become a great deal more familiar in the future.

★ *2* ★

WE BERTHED AT YOKOHAMA ON A POURING WET NIGHT IN OCTOBER. The customs examination on entering Japan is always severe, and particular attention is paid to the traveller's taste in books. I was doing my best to explain why I had arrived with several hundred volumes when a young man from the Foreign Office was announced. In Japan everybody and everything is rigidly graded, and of course the Japanese Customs Department stands much lower in the official hierarchy than the Foreign Office. Nevertheless the young man bowed low to the Customs Inspector before presenting his visiting card, waiting for it to take effect. It produced, of course, a much lower and more obsequious bow, and then a string of apologies, followed by the rapid chalking of my boxes. I was now free to leave the boat, and my Foreign Office friend, having other arrivals to greet, handed me over to Professor Bo, who was waiting on the quay. The Professor was the dean of the English department at the University where I was to teach and had spent some years in England. He seemed to have nothing to say, however, and answered all my own attempts to start a conversation with a curt monosyllable. In a final effort to thaw him I took out my cigarette case and offered it to him. "Thank you; no," he said, "I am a Christian." I should in fairness add that of the many thousands of Christians in Japan only a very small minority feel that their religious views demand complete abstention from alcohol and tobacco.

We made the train journey up to Tokyo (it takes about thirty minutes) in almost complete silence, and after seeing me to the Imperial Hotel, where I was to stay for the time being, the Professor took his leave, saying that he would call me up on the following morning and give me my instructions.

THE IMPERIAL HOTEL, TOKYO

★ 3 ★

THE IMPERIAL HOTEL IN TOKYO IS WORTH A FEW WORDS OF DESCRIPTION since it is the usual meeting place of diplomats, international crooks and other foreigners living in the capital. The position it occupies in the social life of the city is very much like that which the Hotel Adlon in Berlin used to have in the early days of the Hitler régime. It was designed by Frank Lloyd Wright, one of America's foremost architects, and is without doubt one of the most unsuitably constructed buildings in the world. Abnormally low ceilings make the rooms excessively hot in summer, while the maze of useless passages becomes bitterly cold and draughty in winter; but if one disregards its function and looks upon it merely as an abstract design it is not unpleasing. It was one of the first buildings in Tokyo to be built on earthquake-proof principles, and one of the few large buildings to escape damage in the disaster of 1923. I have myself been inside it during a slight earthquake, and can vouch for the fact that, resting on a bed of semi-liquid mud instead of being built on solid foundations like a normal building, it shakes like a jelly, even in quite a mild shock, but it does not fall down. Finally, I may add that since the majority of the Imperial Hotel Company's shares are held by the Imperial Family, guests are expected to observe the strictest propriety. What this means in actual practice is that while no objection is raised to gentlemen entertaining foreign ladies in their rooms, they are not permitted to offer similar hospitality to ladies of the country. Until Japan came into the war the Hotel was patronized almost exclusively by foreigners and Japanese that had been educated abroad, a type that is often more Western than any Westerner.

True to his word the Professor rang me up at half-past six (the Japanese are early risers) the following morning; but I never got his message. It so happened that among the guests staying in the hotel was another John Morris, a well-known American journalist. It appeared that the other Mr. John Morris had been making something of a night of it and had not retired before about 3 a.m. He did not, therefore, appreciate being rung up in the early hours of the morning by an unknown Japanese professor who told him he would call for him at eight. I never discovered the exact wording of his reply, but when the professor came to collect me just as I was thinking of getting out of bed he was unmistakably registering disapproval, and it was some weeks before I was able to convince him that I was in reality quite blameless.

MY LECTURES AT THE UNIVERSITY WERE NOT DUE TO COMMENCE FOR several weeks. In the meantime the housing question had to be settled. The China war had prevented the building of new houses in Tokyo for several years, and, as always happens in wartime, the population of the capital had increased considerably. Finding an empty house in Tokyo in those days was about as difficult as it is to find a furnished flat in London to-day. I was forced to decide between a feudal mansion of twenty rooms, with a truly magnificent garden and a bathroom big enough to swim in, and a tiny Japanese house which was inconveniently small. Although I did not know it at the time, the mansion (at a ridiculously low rental) was only available because no Japanese would live there, it having at one time been a favourite locale for the carrying out of political assassinations. As a matter of fact this would not have deterred me; what I was afraid of was the expense of running so large an establishment. I always regretted not having taken the bigger house; but at the time I had no idea how very inexpensive living was (and, comparatively, still is) in Japan.

I decided, then, to take the smaller house. It was at No. 2 of 3 Chome, Sakae-dori, Shibuya-ku, Tokyo, which translated into plain English means " The Second House in the Third Block of the Street of Prosperity in the Persimmon-Valley Ward of Tokyo." It was situated in what is fast becoming a fashionable district, about twenty minutes from the centre of the city by bus or underground. The windows of the upstairs room looked out on to the back of one of the less expensive of Tokyo's Geisha quarters, and often at night I would fall asleep to the doleful strains of the *Samisen*, punctuated by bursts of drunken laughter, from these pleasure houses on the rising ground across the street.

I have said that my house was Number Two. So, as a matter of fact, was the one next door. The system of numbering houses in Japan is quite peculiar; so much so that a brief description of it is a good introduction to the complexities of Japanese life. Every street is divided into blocks, a block being merely an area of land the property of one individual or company. The houses in any one block are numbered as they are built, irrespective of their position within it. Should the block happen to be a large one, the house numbered One may be at one end of the street, that numbered Two at the other. Moreover, should several new houses be built on a site formerly occupied by one, each retains the number assigned to the original house, so that it is common to find several houses in one street all with the same number. In actual fact a friend of mine lived in a street in which eleven other houses had the same number as his own. On the other hand, when one house has been built upon a site formerly occupied by several, you get the opposite result. Thus, my friend Dr. Sanki Ichikawa, Professor of English in the Tokyo Imperial University, lived in a house that was numbered officially as 25 to 30; but this latter state of affairs is rare. To add further to the confusion, the arrangement of the blocks themselves does not conform to any plan, so that in practice one often finds block Number Six, for instance, adjacent to block Number Ten. As a slight concession to the bemused citizen, street maps are generally found at the entrance to each district; but since inclusion in the map is dependent upon the voluntary payment of a small annual fee, it does not follow that the particular house for which one is patiently searching appears in the plan. The reader can perhaps now realize that one of the commonest sights in Tokyo is that of harassed people wandering disconsolately up and down a street, vainly searching for some house in which they have been invited to dine. This possibly explains the fact that, unless one lived in the Embassy quarter, where the houses are easy to find, an invitation to dine at eight o'clock at an unfamiliar house was always understood as meaning that one would arrive at any time between seven and nine o'clock. The Japanese are extremely vague about time when social engagements are concerned.

My house was typical of those occupied by the middle and lower classes in Tokyo. One could, in fact, say that of Tokyo's seven million or so inhabitants about ninety per cent live in houses of similar pattern, the only difference being one of size. The remaining ten per cent live either in somewhat squalid Apartment Houses, the Japanese equivalent of the modern block of flats, or in so-called Foreign Houses, which are homes of the sort that one finds anywhere in Europe or America. The rows of sordid little houses or semi-detached villas that so disfigure our own towns are unknown in Japan. Every house, even in the meanest quarter, stands alone and in its own garden. The garden may be only a few yards square but

FINDING A HOUSE

it will invariably be arranged with that peculiar Japanese skill for making much of little. Tokyo has often been described as a purely industrial city, which indeed it is; but seen from the air it is green, utterly different from any of the cities of Europe.

My own house was built of wood, lath and plaster, but unlike a European house it had no solid foundations. This mode of building is prevalent everywhere in Japan and permits of a house being moved from one place to another. The ground floor contained one large room, but this could be divided into two or more rooms by the sliding forward of partitions. These partitions, which are made of paper on a light wooden foundation, are one of the most outstanding features of a Japanese home and have given rise to the common belief that the Japanese live in what are often referred to as paper houses.

Japanese houses have certain obvious advantages in that one can arrange the rooms as one wishes. There is, on the other hand, an entire lack of privacy, for every word spoken in the drawing-room can be heard by the cook on the other side of the screen.

The floor of a Japanese house is covered entirely by mats about three inches thick, which fit into slots in the wooden floorboards. These mats are of a standard size and a room is described as being of so many mats in size. No other floor covering is used, and in a Japanese household no distinction is made between the uses to which the various rooms in the house are put. There is no furniture, other than low tables which are brought in as required, and cushions and bedding are laid on the floor when wanted. In view of the fact that the mats are thick and springy they are extremely comfortable and warm to sleep upon, but the chief advantage of this system is that the number of guests one can accommodate for the night is limited, not by the number of one's beds or rooms, but only by the amount of one's bedding. Thus in the tiniest Japanese house it is possible to accommodate a dozen people without discomfort. During the daytime bedding is rolled up and stored in cupboards let into the wall.

There are no pictures on the walls, but every Japanese room contains in one corner what is known as a *tokonoma* or alcove which is slightly raised above the level of the floor. On the back wall of this a hanging picture or scroll is usually displayed and in front of it is placed some work of art, a piece of porcelain or bronze for instance, or a vase of flowers. The space immediately in front of the *tokonoma* is the place of honour and the principal guest at a meal is usually seated with his back to it.

The Japanese bath needs a word of description, since it is one of the most pleasant features of Japanese life. It consists of a wooden tub shaped liked an oval barrel in which the bather squats with his knees drawn up to his chin, only his head protruding from the water. The water is warmed by a small fire or gas-burner underneath the bath and it is the custom to bathe in water which is practically boiling. Very few Europeans acquire the habit of bathing *à la japonaise*, but personally I found it exceedingly agreeable, the trick being to take a deep breath and plunge in up to the neck before the boiling water has time to affect any particular part of the body. If one keeps perfectly quiet and does not move one's limbs about the heat is scarcely felt, but after half an hour or so one emerges feeling like a cross between Haroun Al Raschid and a boiled lobster. The Japanese have always been famed for their cleanliness. It should be remembered, however, that in Japan the bath performs a dual purpose, since the only form of heating in winter is a small charcoal brazier. Some of the older houses do not contain bathrooms of their own, but in Tokyo alone there are some thousands of public bath houses; there is, in fact, one in nearly every street, where for a sum of approximately twopence one can bathe, have one's back scrubbed, and hear all the latest gossip.

Shortly after moving into my house I happened to be alone one day when there was a ring at the door. I hastened to see who it was and found myself confronted by a gentleman in a corduroy uniform wearing white cotton gloves. He brandished a book of tickets in my face and let out a spate of Japanese of which, of course, I was unable to understand one word. My next-door neighbour, who happened also to be my landlord, spoke English, however, quite well, and I trotted in to ask his help. It appeared that my servant, in handing over the tickets in return for which one's lavatory is cleaned, had given too many, payment apparently being demanded by weight. Many people have wondered why, when Tokyo was re-built after the big earthquake in 1923, it was not given a system of modern sanitation. The reason is that the rice-fields are fertilized exclusively by human excrement, for which, apparently there is no satisfactory chemical substitute. As a French writer has truly said: *La base de l'économie japonaise, c'est la merde.* Incidentally, the gentlemen with the white gloves invariably chose to carry out their functions at the very time when one had a luncheon party, which entailed the burning of many sticks of incense.

Upstairs was a room similar to but slightly smaller than the one below; this I used as a bedroom, furnishing it in ordinary European style.

Before leaving the subject of houses, I must just mention my so-called "foreign style" room. To possess such a room has become in modern Japan a sign of culture. These usually take the form of

CONCERNING THE TELEPHONE

a plain box-like erection fastened on to one end of the ordinary Japanese house. The floor is of wood and the furniture of European pattern. It is in the "foreign room" that a Japanese will usually receive his foreign guests; but apart from this the foreign room is little used except as a repository for such things as pianos, tables, chairs, and other odd items of foreign "culture" which the family gradually acquires. My own I fitted up with bookshelves and had intended to use as a study, but owing to the fact that its thin roof and walls made it unbearably hot in summer and as unbearably cold in winter I used it only as a store-room. So thin were its walls that when the Post Office engineers came to fix my telephone I noticed that the man in charge was able to lead the wire into the room merely by pushing his finger through the wall.

★ 5 ★

OBTAINING A TELEPHONE IS NOT THE EASY MATTER IT IS IN MOST OTHER countries, and often entails waiting for four or five years unless one has recourse to the black market. I only got one myself because of my connection with the Foreign Office, and often wished that I had not exercised my privilege. Telephones are still so scarce in private houses that it is an unwritten law that when anyone is lucky or rich enough to obtain one the use of it shall be extended to his neighbours. There were times when the queue in my small study was like one outside a public call-box, and the cook would often have to run down the street to summon someone when she was in the midst of preparing a meal. The Japanese themselves do not find this custom irritating; it is a part of their way of life, and a good example of their lack of feeling for the privacy of the individual. But I felt that things were going a bit far when I discovered that one of my neighbours actually had my telephone number printed on his visiting card.

I have said that obtaining a telephone is not easy in Japan, and the reasons for this throw an interesting light on Japanese methods. As in most other countries, the Japanese telephone system is a government department. When it was first introduced, however, the necessary capital was obtained by means of public subscription in the same way as an ordinary government loan. In this case, however, subscribers did not take up stock but bought telephones, together with their attached exchange numbers. Most of the original subscribers were government officials and not a few of them bought surplus telephones which they afterwards let out on hire. Some years ago Mr. Bell, the famous American telephone engineer, was invited to visit Japan and modernize the system. He evolved a plan by which it would have been possible for practically every house to have its own telephone at a negligible cost. It was approved in theory; but when it came to putting it into practice, vested interests won. Government officials are human in that they do not like to be deprived of any source of profit.

At the present time the only way to obtain a telephone is to buy one. The price for this has been fixed by the government as one thousand yen (roughly £70). In actual practice, however, no owner will sell at this price, and the only method of getting hold of a telephone is to buy one on the black market, at a cost of three or four times the government price. What an instrument will actually fetch depends largely upon the exchange number, for the Japanese, for all their modernity, are extremely superstitious where numbers are concerned, and will pay a high price for a number that is considered lucky. Any increasing number, 3579 for instance, is lucky since it betokens prosperity, and a decreasing number is equally disliked. But the highest prices are paid for numbers which can be read with a double meaning. Thus a well-known bookseller in Tokyo has the telephone number 3746, which is pronounced in Japanese as *mi-na-yo-mu*; but if the syllables are joined so as to read *Mina-yomu* the phrase means "Everybody reads." Another number famous in Tokyo is 2372 (*ni-san-na-ni*), which in its other form is read as *Nisan Nani?* *Nisan* is the form of address used by Geisha to their customers and *nani* means what. The whole phrase may thus be translated as "What can I do for you, sir?" This number has been secured by a very famous restaurant. Other numbers are equally unlucky. Nobody wants the number 1564 (*hito-go-ro-shi*), which can also mean "man gets murdered"; and there is the well-known story, probably apocryphal, of the hospital which never got any patients. Its telephone number was 3786 (*mi-na-ya-mu*), which in ordinary language is read as "Everybody becomes ill."

ENGAGING A SERVANT

★ 6 ★

IT WAS NOT UNTIL THE BEGINNING OF DECEMBER THAT MY HOUSE WAS ready for me. The previous occupant, Forrest Garnett, an American teacher of dancing who had formerly been with Ruth St. Denis and Ted Shawn, had tastes in decoration that did not accord with mine. He had had the walls papered with a dull silver fabric across which moons, stars and other zodiacal designs sprawled, so that with its dim lighting the living room looked more like a soothsayer's parlour than a home. I bought a real Japanese paper, hand made. It was cream-coloured, its plain surface broken up by pieces of silk fluff which were embedded in it without any sort of pattern. The furniture, which I designed myself, was made by a local carpenter. It was of a plain, unpolished wood, not unlike oak, and upholstered in old-gold tapestry. It is customary when a new tenant moves into a house, that the landlord shall furnish him with new mats, and as soon as this had been done I gave up my room at the hotel.

I had engaged a servant on the recommendation of one of my English colleagues, who had previously employed him in some sort of secretarial capacity on account of his knowledge of English. The newcomer to any oriental country has always to buy his experience, but on this occasion I think I was more than usually unfortunate. As I did not at the time know more than a word or two of Japanese I was entirely in the hands of this wretch. That he was no more able to cook than I can was a fault I could have borne; but he was also dishonest and fast becoming a dipsomaniac. This latter weakness he concealed admirably at first, but at the end of a fortnight he passed completely out for three whole days. In normal times I should have been able to carry on somehow or other; but the New Year is a time of celebration in Japan and everything becomes disorganized. The shops close for five whole days, as indeed do many of the restaurants; it is almost impossible to get a meal outside one's home and tradesmen do not call for orders. Most foreigners take the line of least resistance and go away to one or other of the hotels in the country, where life is less disturbed. Some of the acquaintances I had made had warned me vaguely that it was advisable to be away from the capital at this time of the year; but I had so recently arrived in the country that I had no one to go with; also, I wanted to spend the vacation getting the house really ship-shape. Anyhow, there I was with a drunken servant on my hands and no available friend from whom to beg a meal. I subsisted largely on tea and toast, eating my meals, such as they were, with a Japanese grammar propped against the teapot; obviously it was necessary to become linguistically independent at the earliest possible moment. Whenever I tried to rouse the man he became insulting, and I can at least give him credit for having a better command of English invective than I have. In one of his more lucid moments he informed me that he disliked Europeans, the reason being that they smelt like camels. When at last he had come back to himself he was tearfully apologetic, and for the time being I had no choice but to tolerate him. During the next few weeks he alternated between perfect sobriety, when he was freezingly polite, and an unconsciousness so complete that on one occasion I thought he had died. The end came at about three o'clock one morning when I was suddenly awakened by the sound of breaking crockery. I slipped on a dressing-gown and hurried downstairs to see what was happening. It appeared that in groping his way through the kitchen entrance to his bedroom he had caught hold of the dresser and pulled it away from the wall. I shoved him into his room and flung a covering over him, but fifteen minutes later he was back in the kitchen, apparently smashing up what was left of the china. I am not normally pugilistic, but on this occasion I lost my temper and knocked him completely out. When I gave him notice the following day he tried to blackmail me, so I immediately telephoned to the police. The Japanese Police can be both irritating and annoying, but in cases of this sort they are extremely helpful. Against any attempt at blackmail they are only too willing to afford the utmost protection. They came to my aid at once and removed my factotum, who was by now thoroughly frightened, for any Japanese who arouses the suspicion of the police becomes a marked man for the rest of his life. This, too, as I now learnt, was by no means his first encounter with the police, who were, in fact, quite glad to have the opportunity of offering him a little more government hospitality. When I last heard of him he was employed as a tout for a restaurant of somewhat doubtful reputation. I am glad to say that he was certainly not a typical Japanese servant. Although possessed of a Japanese name and completely Japanese in appearance, he was as a matter of fact an Eurasian, but I did not know this until the police told me later. Educated in Ceylon (which accounted for his exceptional knowledge of English), he was the son of a German. His father had lived in Ceylon for many years, had become a Buddhist priest and acquired British nationality. The son had been born when the father was on a pilgrimage to Japan. The fruit of a temporary liaison, he was, in fact, what in his more drunken moments he had often called me.

Well, here I was! Servantless and in a pretty plight. The table was a litter of empty milk bottles, crumbs and half-opened tins. It had also turned bitterly cold, and snow was falling. To add to my discomfort, too, a constant stream of tradesmen came to my door so that I was perpetually running in and out of the neighbouring house in order to get my landlord to interpret. It is usual in Japan to pay one's tradesmen monthly, but in the case of regular customers a certain amount of latitude is, of course, allowed. It is, however, the rule all over Japan to settle one's debts by the 31st December. If one can avoid doing this there is no legal obligation to pay before the end of the following year. As a matter of fact I had been paying my bills weekly, and it was only now that I realized that the money which I had handed over to my servant for this purpose had gone not to the tradesmen but into his own pocket.

For the time being there was nothing for it but to leave the house. The university term was about to commence and I had lectures to prepare. It was impossible to work at home, for not only was the unheated house unbearably cold, but I was spending the greater part of the day in trying, inefficiently, to keep it in some sort of order. Thus after three months in Tokyo I found myself back again in the Imperial Hotel.

A few days later the "treasure" appeared. She was an elderly widow and had been cook to a French family for many years. Except for the words for things used in the kitchen, she knew no English, but had managed to pick up a slight smattering of French. Until such time as I was able to make myself understood in Japanese we conversed in a strange jargon, compounded of all three languages, which I doubt if anyone except our two selves could have understood. She was the best servant I have ever had, and the most faithful. Even after war came she refused to leave me, though this meant spending long hours waiting in the food queues and bearing the taunts of neighbouring servants, who reviled her for working for an enemy. She remained with me right to the end, a model of tact and patience, especially when dealing with the police and other snoopers on their periodical visits. She rose to her greatest heights, I think, in accepting the extra pound of sugar which was issued to celebrate the fall of Singapore, while at the same time disobeying the government order that every house should display the national flag as an outward sign of rejoicing. I only hope that she is not now suffering for her faithfulness.

JAPANESE FOOD

★ 7 ★

I USED TO GO QUITE OFTEN TO JAPANESE RESTAURANTS, BUT I CANNOT say that I ever got to like the food since a purely Japanese meal, apart from rice, consists almost entirely of various kinds of fish, many of which are eaten raw. I cannot say how the number of Tokyo's restaurants compares with the number of its inhabitants, but it always seemed that it contained more eating houses of one kind and another than any other city that I know. There are certain quarters where every house is a restaurant, and in no part of the town does one have to go far to find one. This is partly due to the fact that the Japanese do not entertain much in their own houses; but since the war the use of restaurants has increased tremendously, as indeed it has with us, in order to eke out home rations.

The best restaurants are very small; many of them cannot accommodate more than a dozen guests at a time. Not a few are hidden away in dark little alleys and are difficult to discover. A foreigner has little chance of enjoying the more exclusive ones unless guided to them by a Japanese friend. Everybody has, I suppose, his own peculiarities, and one of mine is that I always like to know what I am eating, with which is coupled an unfortunate lack of courage in being able to tackle exotic foods. The first time I was taken to have a Japanese meal we started with slices of raw pink fish, which made me feel definitely sick. These were followed by soup which looked and tasted like a scoopful of deep-sea water heated up. Floating about in it were bits of assorted seaweed (for which the Japanese have a passion), and various small bi-valvular objects, half detached from their shells, and other small marine creatures. I was able to deal with this by drinking off the liquid and leaving the garnitures at the bottom of the cup. The taste was not actually unpleasant, but I felt none the less as though I was turning into an aquarium. Soup was followed by a cooked dish, the nature of which I was quite unable to determine. It tasted rather like an oily variety of pork, but yet was obviously not meat. Seeing my perplexity my host attempted to explain, but unfortunately his English had got a bit rusty. "It is a long and writhing creature," he said, "the exact name of which I have forgotten." And then after a pause, "Ah, yes," he continued, "now I recall its name. It is what you call a serpent." It transpired, however, that we were not eating snakes but eels. This is

JAPANESE FOOD

one of the greatest of all Japanese delicacies; but in view of my first unfortunate experience with it I was never able to overcome my original nausea. The eel was followed by further varieties of fish and finished in the traditional manner with rice and tea. Rice, incidentally, is not generally eaten with other things but comes at the end of the meal, so that one can go on eating bowl after bowl until hunger is completely satisfied.

Most of the good restaurants specialize in certain dishes. There are, for instance, hundreds of restaurants that devote themselves to the eel in various guises, while others specialize in such fare as bees or bull frogs. I never had the courage to try the latter, which are kept alive in a pool beneath the counter. A friend of mine said, however, that they were delicious and tasted rather like chicken. He also added that they were the size of a well-fed lap-dog and had protruding eyes the size of golf balls, and that when the chef had succeeded in dragging one out of the pool and placed it on the counter, prior to knocking it on the head, it was highly desirable to look the other way since the creature goggled in the most unpleasant manner; it did almost everything except bark. I must in fairness add that many foreigners acquire a great fondness for all kinds of Japanese food. That I was never able to do so is doubtless due to some psychological factor, but I did reach the stage of being able to tackle raw fish without being actually sick.

There are, however, two Japanese dishes which the most hidebound can eat with pleasure. The first of these is known as *Sukiyaki*, strips of beef cooked with vegetables on a small brazier, generally electric, which is placed in front of the guests, who attend to the cooking themselves. The other is known as *Tempura*, and consists of various kinds of shell-fish, lobsters, prawns and so on, fried in batter and served very hot. It is delicious.

A good Japanese meal consists of a great number of courses, but many of these contain hardly a mouthful of food. The result is that the average foreigner rises still feeling hungry, for very few have the Japanese capacity for consuming large quantities of rice at the end. So much for the purely gastronomic point of view.

But there is also an æsthetic side to the matter, and a great part of the pleasure to be derived from eating in famous restaurants lies not so much in the actual food as in admiring the varied assortment of plates and bowls in which it is served, and the decoration of the room. The utensils are nearly always extremely beautiful and are often the work of famous artists. In the really good restaurants there is no public dining-room, but only a series of private rooms. These can normally accommodate about four persons in comfort, but, as in the case of a Japanese house, it is always possible to throw two or three rooms into one by merely sliding away the partitions. In a purely Japanese restaurant there is, of course, no furniture other than the low tables off which one eats, and, as in a Japanese house, shoes are discarded in the vestibule.

There is one famous restaurant in Tokyo known as the *Gajo-en* which is to provincial Japanese what any of the bigger Lyons Corner Houses are to English country visitors. It is famous chiefly for its size and for the astonishing display of " art " which adorns its walls. It is much patronized by the rich and uncultured and specialises in providing rather ostentatious wedding banquets. It prides itself particularly on being able to accommodate a thousand guests in the principal room. This is built in the form of a very long but wide corridor with five hundred little tables on one side and another five hundred on the other. I never saw it filled with guests; but when empty it reminded me of one of the halls in a large Tibetan monastery.

The restaurant is entered through an artificial grotto which strikes the keynote, as it were, of the whole building. The rocks of which it is composed are " bigger and better " than in any natural grotto; in fact the aim of the proprietor has been to make the whole place " bigger and better " than any similar institution in Japan. Guides await one in the hall, for it is considered necessary first to undertake a conducted tour of the building. There must be nearly a mile of corridors, every square inch of which is covered with pictures, most of them apparently chosen for their size. Enormous goggling Geisha by the square foot stand side by side with gigantic cows and outsize prawns and lobsters; anything commends itself that is big. A Japanese friend of mine rightly said: " It is necessary to see the *Gajo-en* in order to realize the depths to which our art can sink."

There are special rooms where only Chinese food is served, and many in which other foreign dishes are obtainable. The largest of the " foreign rooms " is furnished with a huge red lacquer table and chairs and gives the impression that it was designed for a film setting. It looks exactly like the traditional Hollywood conception of an oriental banqueting hall. But the pride of the whole restaurant is the lavatories, which came at the end of our conducted tour. These were such as to make even a film star envious, for into their construction there entered onyx and mother-of-pearl. It seemed almost a desecration to put them to use, but we could hardly turn a deaf ear to the urgent and reiterated " Please, please " of our guide. She then took us into the toilets, which were constructed of similar material. They were the most luxurious I have ever seen, and it was odd to find them devoid of paper. As a matter of fact this is seldom provided in Japan since everyone carries about his own supply.

In addition to its numerous eating rooms, the *Gajo-en* also contains a number of consecrated shrines and temples, so that if it is desired to have a religious wedding ceremony this can be carried out on the premises. For this purpose the restaurant has its resident staff of priests. Although the matter is not actually mentioned in the prospectus, I do not doubt that, if necessary, even a bride could be provided.

In addition to the thousands of purely Japanese restaurants in Tokyo there are also large numbers of so-called foreign eating houses. In three or four famous ones the cooking is in fact European and excellent; in the others it answers to the Japanese conception of what occidental food should be. They have done to our food what they have done to our language; assimilated odds and ends and adapted them to their own needs. The majority of these places are named after well known London and New York restaurants. Thus there is in Tokyo a Scott's, the walls of which are decorated with menus from its famous prototype, and a Rainbow Grill, where, unlike the New York original, the most highly priced meal costs rather less than half an American dollar. There is a regular chain of Florida Kitchens and a host of other places which specialize in various American dishes, waffles, strawberry shortcake, and so on; but everything is a pale and sickly copy of the original. The art of making good coffee is the one thing the Japanese have really mastered; until the war put a stop to all supplies, it was as easily obtainable as it is in New York. At the time I left, however, it had deteriorated into an *ersatz* mixture (made largely from soya beans) which tasted like an infusion of sawdust.

The cheaper places are patronized chiefly by the student class. The food obtainable in them is definitely inferior to that provided in Japanese restaurants at a similar price; but they are popular because they would seem to fulfil some sort of psychological need. There is a desire not only to absorb western culture, but also to move in a western atmosphere. It is only the fortunate few who can afford to spend some years in a foreign country, and these restaurants, together with the cinema, are the next best substitute for the less fortunate majority. There was to me something pathetic about them; the spectacle of a people torn between two ways of living is always discomforting, and in these places one sensed the conflict at its worst.

The more expensive foreign restaurants are popular even with the more old-fashioned type of Japanese. One of the reasons for this

JAPANESE DRESS

is that even in the best of them, the food is very much cheaper than it is in a Japanese restaurant of similar class. In the New Grand, for instance, which is the best of its type in Tokyo, one could formerly get an excellent meal for the equivalent of six shillings, and there, except for drinks and tips, the matter ended. But in a Japanese restaurant of similar class there are so many extras whch are by custom considered an indispensable part of the meal; a private room, Geisha, and a car (provided by the restaurant) to take each of the guests home. The bill for quite a small dinner in a place of this sort can easily amount to two or three pounds a head, so that it is not difficult to understand why the foreign-style restaurants have now become so popular, especially for entertaining, with all classes of Japanese.

I OFTEN WONDERED WHY THE JAPANESE HAVE SUCH A PASSION FOR Occidental clothing, which does not become them. Even the most insignificant looking Japanese wears an air of natural nobility when in a kimono; there is something of the dark tiger about him, whereas in Western dress he makes a rather pathetic imitation of a European.

It is significant of the Japanese mind that the wearing of the national dress is forbidden at Court, and no member of the Imperial family ever appears in public in anything except Western attire. The result of this is that the European morning coat, striped trousers and top-hat have become the usual costume for all formal occasions. Even the humblest government official possesses the necessary outfit, and I would wager that there are more morning coats in Japan than in any other country in the world. They are worn on every ceremonial occasion; school speech-days, weddings, funerals, even official calls on a superior, require the wearing of morning dress. And it need hardly be said that no Japanese would appear to make his bow before the Emperor's photograph on the numerous occasions when it is ceremonially displayed without being thus attired.

The Japanese take great pride in their genius for adaptation, and this is certainly in evidence with the foreign clothes they wear. Only high government officials and those who have travelled abroad, wear a top-hat with morning dress. Others put on anything that happens to be at hand, more often than not an ordinary cloth cap, or even a béret. Black shoes are not considered a necessary accompaniment. Indeed I have even seen a man wearing white tennis shoes with a morning coat. The American preference for a belt in place of braces has found widespread favour in Japan, and this article is more often than not visible below the wearer's waistcoat.

It is the custom everywhere in Japan to remove one's shoes before entering the house and leave them in the hall. Until one becomes used to it one finds it troublesome to take them off and put them on again several times a day, but the custom is an excellent one and enables Japanese houses to be kept very much cleaner than ours. It has one disadvantage, however: it causes nearly all Japanese to wear shoes several times too large, since this enables them to kick them off without having to untie the laces. This is certainly convenient, but it does not make for elegance. Moreover, it is responsible for the peculiar shuffling gait so commonly seen in Japanese when wearing Western dress.

Shoes are even removed before entering a Japanese-style restaurant, and when the first big department stores were opened in Tokyo no customer was allowed in until he had given up his shoes in exchange for a pair of soft slippers. But in the case of the shops the custom was discontinued after the big earthquake of 1923. It is still continued in the auditoriums of schools and universities, and it always gave me a malicious pleasure on important speech-days to see the row of embassy representatives seated on the dais. They would invariably be clad down to the ankles as though for a Whitehall Conference, but there the resemblance ended for their feet would be thrust into shabby felt slippers. I do not know if that was the intention, but the Japanese could hardly have hit on a better method of pricking the bubble of ambassadorial pomposity; no man can look dignified on a public platform when he is wearing a pair of old carpet slippers with his morning outfit.

Bowler-hats are also popular, but strangely enough they are worn only with a Japanese kimono, and never with a Western suit. But the strangest sight I saw during the whole of my time in Japan was a man walking along the street clad only in a suit of woollen underclothing and a hard felt hat. His appearance did not attract the slightest attention. One can, in fact, wear almost any combination of Western attire, however incongruous, but woe betide the foreigner who appears in a Japanese kimono unless every detail of his dress is strictly correct; he will immediately arouse the politely concealed laughter and comment of any Japanese who happen to see him.

The wearing of Japanese dress is hedged about with formality. There is no variation in the actual cut and shape of a kimono, but the pattern of the material is dependent upon the age of the wearer. Soon after I arrived in the country I went to a shop to choose some material to be made up into summer kimonos. Foreigners do not often wear Japanese dress in public, but many do so at the seaside resorts or in the privacy of their own homes, since a collar and tie are irksome in the humid Japanese summer. I had chosen what I thought was a quiet and inoffensive pattern and asked the shopman to have the material made up. He seemed to be slightly worried and I finally asked him if anything was wrong. "Excuse me, sir," he said, " but are the kimonos for your esteemed self ? "—" But yes," I replied, " for whom else should they be ? "—" Forgive me for my rudeness," he continued, " but the patterns you have chosen are only suitable for a youth. For a dignified gentleman of your advanced years I would venture to recommend something slightly different."

Usage demands that the older the wearer the smaller shall be the pattern and the more drab the colour of the material. This applies both to men and women, with the result that it is always possible to gauge at least the approximate age of any woman when she is wearing her national dress, for in no circumstances whatever would she appear in a kimono unsuited to her years. In the days when tourists were still in existence, it was a source of amusement to Japanese women to see middle-aged and even elderly foreigners investing in the sort of brightly coloured kimonos that should only properly be worn by girls of under twenty.

In extreme old age the kimonos worn by both sexes are approximately the same. This sometimes makes it difficult to distinguish between a man and a woman, especially if the latter is a widow for widows often wear their hair cropped short. This custom, which used to be universal, comes as a reminder of the olden days when a woman was expected to enter a nunnery on the death of her husband.

There has been a tendency in quite recent times for men to return to the wearing of Japanese dress. This is due partly to the present-day outburst of nationalism, and partly to the difficulty of obtaining imported materials. A great deal of cloth is manufactured in Japan in normal times, but in quality it cannot be compared with the best foreign material, and, since the war, even the home-made stuff has been practically unobtainable, as the wool and cotton for its manufacture have all to be imported.

The custom of wearing foreign dress in Japan has become almost universal among the male population, and is explained by the fact that the kimono is unsuited to a modern business life. Moreover good silk kimonos are extremely expensive, and certainly the long hanging sleeves are inconvenient when working in an office. But most men change into their national dress after returning home in the evening; it is not possible to sit at one's ease on the floor when wearing a pair of European trousers.

The craze for foreign dress has not spread nearly so much among the women. The great majority cling to their national costume, and very becoming it is! But whether the Japanese woman's preference for the kimono is due to innate female conservatism, or whether it comes from the realization that foreign dress does not suit her I have never been able to discover. Certain it is, however, that the number of Japanese women who are able to look well in Western costume is extremely limited. For this there are definite reasons, and they are largely bound up with the traditional Japanese idea of feminine grace, although the social customs of the country have also something to do with the matter.

Japanese babies are usually carried about papoose fashion on their mother's or nurse's backs, their legs straddling the waist of the person carrying them. The result of this practice is that nearly all Japanese are to some extent bow-legged, especially the women, as they lead a less athletic life. Moreover, the custom of sitting on chairs is not yet universal, and constant squatting on the floor is not conducive to the growth of shapely lower limbs. The Japanese themselves realize this and have an expression *daikon-ashi*, meaning "legs like a giant radish." Bow-legged girls are at a distinct disadvantage when they wear a costume which brings these features into prominence. It is considered graceful in a woman to walk with small mincing steps, if possible keeping her knees touching each other. I have been told that geisha are trained to walk in this way by holding a visiting card between the knees. But a bow-legged woman can only do this by turning in her toes. Fortunately, Japanese men find this position of the feet captivating. As for me, I always thought it extremely ungraceful, but these things, I suppose, are matters of taste. There is no doubt that the Japanese idea of physical beauty is very different from ours.

The war has affected women's dress in Japan quite as much as in England. The cut and shape of the kimono never change, but in peace time fashion dictated a constant change in the pattern printed on the material used; thus a large iris pattern might be the fashion one year, a cubist design the next. This is all now changed, and the Japanese woman of to-day is encouraged to make shift with such clothes as she already possesses. Attempts have been made to popularize a utility kimono, a drab olive khaki in colour, but I never saw anybody wearing it. The wearing of expensive and richly-embroidered kimonos is, however, definitely frowned upon, even if they have been in the wearer's possession for years. There is no government regulation about this, but in the last few months before I left it was a common sight to see members of one or other of the numerous Women's Patriotic Societies picketing the streets and remonstrating with any well-dressed women who happened to wander by. Even before the war this practice was not unknown, and I remember a friend, Phyllis Argall, concerning whom I shall have more to say in the last part of this book, telling me that she was once stopped in the street by a Japanese woman and soundly rated for wearing a fur coat. The wearing of such a coat, she was told, was not in accordance with the spirit of the China incident.

Since the war, Japanese women have been forbidden by government to have their hair permanently waved. The reasons given for this are firstly that the custom is Western, and therefore bad, and secondly that it is a waste of time and money. At the same time all forms of make-up, with the exception of the traditional Japanese, are discouraged. Although very few Japanese women habitually wear foreign dress, nearly all of them, except geisha and the very aged, nowadays dress their hair in Western style. The traditional Japanese style of hair-dressing which again varies with age and social position, is not only extremely ugly, but laborious to effect; moreover, it entails sleeping on a wooden pillow in order that the hair shall not become disarranged. It is the custom, however, for a Japanese girl to be married with her hair dressed in the traditional way, but as this is not possible when the hair is worn short, wigs are nowadays usually worn on this occasion. A Japanese style of hair-dressing also calls for a purely Japanese make-up. In this the face and neck are painted dead white with liquid, and on this base a whitish powder is applied, and the lower lip only is rouged. It always seemed to me to give the women a somewhat clownish appearance, and I could never get used to the contrast visible in the line of demarcation at the base of the neck, between the hideous pallor of the painted flesh and the really lovely colour of the natural skin.

★ *9* ★

WHEN I FIRST ARRIVED IN JAPAN I WAS MUCH STRUCK BY THE FACT that very few foreigners spoke the language; of those who did the

THE JAPANESE LANGUAGE

majority seemed to be Germans. It is possible to get on quite comfortably without learning a single word of Japanese, for many of the servant class speak English, and there are still large numbers of Japanese of the upper classes who have been educated abroad. I found that the English community in Tokyo was particularly neglectful of acquiring the language, and regarded the few who differed from them in this respect as eccentrics. I never came across a single member of the British Embassy who was in touch with the new type of Japanese (doubtless not socially prepossessing) which was fast obtaining control of the country. There is evidence that this state of affairs was not peculiar to Japan. Since my return I have learnt that a complacent insularity goes far to explain the failure of so many of our missions.

That the Japanese language is about as hard to conquer as Mount Everest I must freely admit; but, contrary to current notions, it is not particularly difficult to learn to speak it. Unlike most Oriental languages it has no sounds that are difficult to produce, and the construction of sentences is easy. The chief stumbling-block to the European is the almost complete lack of intonation, for it is hard to acquire the habit of speaking in a flat monotonous voice. There are, however, certain other difficulties which are not specifically connected with the actual learning of the language. The foreigner in Japan, although he usually has wide connections (unless he is a diplomat), comes mostly in contact with people who have at least some knowledge of his own language. The Japanese, on the other hand, have few opportunities of speaking with a foreigner in his own tongue, and it is only natural that they should wish to make the most of every chance to practise. This makes it difficult for the foreigner to learn Japanese, especially if he happens to be an Englishman, for of all foreign languages English is the most widely known in Japan. Teachers of English were, in fact, at one time more or less officially discouraged from learning Japanese. One of my predecessors became so good at the language that his services were actually dispensed with for this very reason. With the rise, however, of nationalism in recent years the situation has somewhat changed, and the foreigner who does not now make an effort to learn a little Japanese is looked upon askance. But this brings him to a further difficulty, for sooner or later he is almost bound to find himself called upon to explain to the police the exact reasons for his study. The Japanese police cannot understand that life in a foreign country is not only easier, but much more interesting and pleasant if one can speak the language; in their minds the desire betokens something sinister, the wish to pry into things that should be hidden from all foreigners. Although I never became fluent in the language, I did reach the stage of being able to converse with ease on simple topics, but I was always very careful, when the local policeman made his periodic visit, to appear much less fluent than in fact I was.

To learn to read and write Japanese is, however, quite another matter. The Japanese, having obtained their civilization from China and Korea, were inevitably led to adopt the ideographic system of writing current in those countries. The exact date of its introduction cannot be fixed, but would seem to be somewhere about A.D. 400. Some writers have made much of the fact that in their simple forms many Chinese (and, of course, Japanese) ideographs are pictorial hieroglyphs. There is some truth in this; but it gives the student little help, for he very soon passes beyond the stage when it is possible to trace any pictorial resemblance between the signs and their meaning. The average Japanese, educated up to the secondary standard, has probably learnt from fifteen hundred to two thousand ideographs. This is enough to enable him to read newspapers, magazines, modern novels, and so on. A university graduate, of course, knows considerably more, probably five or six thousand; but even he will have difficulty in reading classical literary Japanese, unless he happens to have made a special study of the subject. The real difficulty lies in the fact that when the reader comes across a word of which he does not know the meaning, he cannot even pronounce it. In a European language any educated person can guess at the approximate meaning of an unfamiliar word; but this is not possible in Japanese seeing that every word has its own separate symbol. There is, moreover, the added difficulty that in Japanese nearly every word can be pronounced in at least two quite different ways, while some have many alternative pronunciations. The reason for this is that most words can be given either the Chinese or Japanese pronunciation, and that there is no absolute rule which governs the choice. The so-called Chinese pronunciation has, by the way, little affinity with the spoken Chinese of to-day; it is the pronunciation of Chinese words as they sounded to Japanese ears at the time when the written language was first adopted. Japanese dictionaries of the written language list, according to their size, from eighteen to sixty thousand ideographs, of which, needless to say, a large proportion are unknown even to the highly educated. Many attempts have been made to limit the number of ideographs for ordinary use, but they have always been unsuccessful. Prior to the outbreak of the China incident in 1937 the *Asahi*, which is the leading Tokyo newspaper, made use of about two thousand ideographs, but this number has been doubled since the war, owing to the necessity for using little-known Chinese place-names. It has been pointed out that a total of some 5,000 basic ideographs would be sufficient for all ordinary purposes, but every scheme put forward to limit the number in use is hotly opposed by the men of letters who, like their fellows in other countries, are apt to be pedants, and to love linguistic difficulties for their own sake. From a literary point of view, too, there is, indeed, something to be said for the present state of affairs, since it enables the learned and fastidious writer to choose his words not only for their sound and meaning, but also for their artistic appearance. This visual element is of particular importance in poetry, and furnishes one of the reasons why it is almost impossible to translate Japanese poetry satisfactorily into English.

During the eighth and ninth centuries there came into use in Japan another system of writing, called *Kana*. This is composed of those parts of the Chinese characters which happened to be most commonly employed. There are two forms of it, called respectively *Kata kana* and *Hira gana*, each containing forty-eight signs. Whereas a Chinese ideograph directly represents a whole word, the *Kana* represents the sounds of which the word is composed, just as our own writing does. But whereas the Roman symbol stands for a letter, the *Kana* symbol stands for a syllable. Modern Japanese writing is a combination of ideographs and *Kana*, the latter being used to indicate the tense of verbs. The *Hira gana* is used for this purpose, while the *Kata kana* is used almost exclusively for the transliteration of foreign words. It would, of course, be possible to do away entirely with ideographs and write only in *Kana*, which is completely phonetic. The great argument against it is that the Japanese language contains numerous homonyms, and that to write it phonetically results in great confusion. This, too, is the reason why the various attempts to introduce the use of the Roman alphabet have never obtained much support.

The Japanese are at present making efforts to introduce their language into the various territories they have conquered, but I do not think they are likely to meet with much success until such time as they simplify it very considerably. Indeed, they themselves find it exceedingly perplexing at times. Take, for instance, the matter of personal names. In Japan an introduction is followed by an exchange of visiting cards, after which there comes a little ceremonial conversation which is designed principally to elicit the manner in which the parties pronounce their respective names. Family names are generally easy; these were not in use in Japan (if we except the nobility) until some eighty years ago, and as a rule they are simple place names. But in the matter of personal names it is the custom, especially among the educated classes, either to select some quite common name and denote it by some little-known ideograph, or to select a rather uncommon name and write it with a well-known ideograph. Thus, to take an example which happens to occur to me at the moment, the simple sign — stands for the figure one. It is a name commonly given to an eldest son. Unfortunately, however, it can be pronounced in about fourteen ways, and seeing it on a visiting card one has not the slightest idea which of the alternative pronunciations the owner affects.[1] This is a very simplified case. It has been my frequent experience to hear two gentlemen, previously unknown to one another, using the utmost ingenuity to avoid displaying their ignorance of the correct pronunciation of each other's names. Some people, whose names are written with little-known ideographs, have on their visiting cards the *Kana* version printed alongside the ideograph as a clue to its pronunciation. This custom is also very commonly adopted in women's magazines (for which there is a great demand in Japan), in some of which the entire text is given with the *Kana* version in a parallel column. Educated women have, of course, as wide a knowledge of the ideographs as men; but the majority of the magazines are written primarily to appeal to women of the working classes, whose written vocabulary is strictly limited. Nowadays, too, in books of a technical nature it is becoming increasingly common to indicate the pronunciation of rarely used ideographs.

Japanese ideographs, like Chinese, are supposed to be written in vertical columns from right to left, although the actual strokes of each separate ideograph are written from left to right. But, unfortunately, no fixed rule is observed and books are sometimes printed in columns which are meant to be read from left to right. On opening a book, however, one soon finds out if one has begun to read from the wrong side of the page; but this inconsistency in other fields raises difficulties which are almost insuperable, sometimes even to the Japanese themselves. The modernization of the country calls for shop-signs, advertisements on hoardings and so on, and it has been found inconvenient to write these in the normal vertical columns. Thus, there has now arisen the custom of writing horizontally as well, and some people write horizontally from right to left, others from left to right. In the case of shop-signs, which usually consist of just a name or some very short slogan, there is no means of telling how to read the sign; often it will have one meaning if read from right to left, another if read in the opposite

[1] The Chinese equivalent of the Oxford English Dictionary devotes no less than 200 pages to this ideograph alone.

direction. A simple example will perhaps make this point clearer. Tamura and Murata are both rather common family names; both are written with the same two ideographs (*ta*, meaning a rice field, and *mura* meaning a village), but, of course, in opposite order. If the word is written vertically there can be no confusion as to which is meant; but if it is printed horizontally and alone, in the form of a shop-sign for instance, there is no means of knowing which of the two alternatives is intended. The height of confusion is reached in the combination of all the various systems in one piece of writing. Absurd as it may seem advertisements are often produced in this manner. Shortly before I left Japan the government issued a command that in writing horizontally the order of words should always be from right to left. The Japanese are, of course, quite used to being dictated to, and generally show complete docility; but in writing their language they seem determined to follow their individual whims. One of my last memories of Tokyo is of a man engaged in repainting a sign. I saw him on my way to the station and noticed that although the arrangement of the words had previously been in accordance with the new government order, he was blocking them out and rewriting them in the opposite direction.

Truly, it is not difficult to understand why few foreigners get far in reading or writing the language of the country. To do so calls for sustained mental and physical effort. There is no short cut to learning the ideographs; each new one must be written out hundreds of times until it is indelibly impressed upon the memory. Even when living in Japan, where one sees ideographs everywhere, it takes more than an average intelligence, and from three to four years of regular study, to acquire a working knowledge of the written language. Outside Japan it naturally takes much longer. In spite of this, however, officers of the British army who before the war were sent to Japan to study the language, were expected to acquire complete proficiency in a maximum period of three years. After this, most of them were returned to their units, where they quickly forgot almost all they had learnt. Here, too, is something that goes far to explain why we know so little about the Japanese, a gap in our knowledge for which we are now paying dearly. Our government has never thought it worth while to offer any inducement to the large numbers of British civilians normally resident in Japan to make an effort to study either the spoken or written language. Other governments, notably the German, have known better.

There are some people, of course, who can never learn to read Japanese. It undoubtedly requires a visual memory of more than normal capacity. Persons of the right endowment can easily be picked out by any competent psychologist. I have often wondered why this simple measure is not adopted by our government. Missionaries to Japan are generally required by their boards to make an intensive study of the language and are recalled if they have not reached a reasonable standard after some three years. It is no disgrace to admit defeat, but in truly Oriental fashion a " face-saving " excuse has been invented for the defeated. They are invalided as sufferers from a disease that appears in no medical text-book; it is called " Japanese head."

My own efforts to acquire the elements of the written language were intense while they lasted but they did not last long. The first two ideographs I attempted were the signs for man (人) and woman (女). There was a good practical reason for this; one of the first things I do in any foreign country is to make quite sure that I know where to go in case of emergency. I soon familiarized myself with these two simple signs, but when I had occasion to enter a place marked (人), to my dismay I found it occupied by several women. I blamed my memory, but wrongly, for I soon discovered that the Japanese are far from pernickety in these matters. I have always thought that we English are unduly squeamish where the natural functions of the body are concerned. But the Japanese go rather too far in the opposite direction: public urination, although in theory it makes the perpetrator of the offence liable to a sixpenny fine, does not arouse the slightest comment, and small children, like the dogs in some of London's more fashionable quarters, are given the freedom of the pavements.

But to return: the study of Japanese writing is fascinating. Every walk in the streets becomes a sort of competition in which one hopes to recognize more ideographs than one did the day before. There was a time when I became so absorbed in this form of amusement that I was in constant danger of being run over; I would become so deep in concentration that I often failed to notice the tram or taxi that was about to bear down upon me. It is not difficult to learn one's first hundred or so ideographs. After that there comes a stage when previously learnt symbols are forgotten at about the same rate that new ones are acquired. I am told that once this stage is passed further progress is comparatively rapid, but I never got beyond it. What caused me to give up was not altogether despair: I found that the constant poring over badly printed characters was affecting my eyesight; even with glasses the ideographs soon started to swim about on the paper.

The Japanese are the most be-spectacled nation in the world. Without doubt the chief reason for this is the nature of the written language, although malnutrition ranks high as a contributory factor. When I once pointed this out to a Japanese friend he agreed with me. "But don't forget," he continued proudly, "that it is also responsible for the fact that we are the biggest manufacturers of spectacles in the world."

Japanese writing should consist of strong bold strokes made with a brush dipped in Chinese ink. Ideographs thus formed are not only extremely beautiful to look at, but do not strain the eyes. It takes many years of practice to make a really good calligrapher, and I am sorry to say that the art is unquestionably declining. To a Japanese, writing takes its place beside painting, and connoisseurs will pay high prices for specimens of the work of famous calligraphers. These usually take the form of classical Chinese poems, and not infrequently their present owners are quite unable to read them. They are prized not as poetry, but as objects of beauty appealing to the eye, and it is for this reason that they serve as decoration and are exhibited in the same way as paintings. The late Sir Ernest Satow, at one time British Ambassador to Japan, became so skilful as a calligrapher that specimens of his work are highly prized by Japanese collectors.

But the printing press and fountain pen between them, if they have not yet actually killed the art of calligraphy, have dealt it a mortal wound, and among the younger generation are many who have never learnt to use the brush with any degree of skill. Newspaper print and the cursive form of the language written with an ordinary pen or pencil have a terrible effect upon the eyesight. Their injuriousness is specially noticeable among the educated. In fact, in one of my classes, consisting of about thirty boys, every single one wore glasses.

★ *10* ★

I MUST NOW GO BACK A LITTLE TO PICK UP THE THREAD OF MY STORY. Well do I remember the bitterly cold November morning in 1938, when I gave my first lecture. This was before I had moved into my house and I left the Imperial Hotel at seven in the morning, for the Japanese are early risers, and classes start at eight o'clock.

I suppose that the word university has for English readers definite associations; it conjures up in the mind a picture of old grey build-

EDUCATION

ings, of pleasant lawns and leisurely study. Nothing could be more different from Oxford and Cambridge than a Japanese University. The one to which I was first attached was small and specialized in the training of teachers of English. Every graduate was, in fact, in duty bound to become, at any rate for his first few years, a teacher in one or other of the thousands of middle schools scattered about Japan. The building was suggestive of a prison rather than a university, and seemed not to have been cleaned since the day it was built. The windows were thick with grime and difficult to open; and I can remember that the broken sash of one of the windows in my classroom was still unmended when I left although I had asked for its repair on my first arrival. There was an iron stove in one corner of the room and a pile of firewood, but never anyone to light it. It is considered bad manners in Japan to wear one's overcoat inside a house but I did not at first know this and used to deliver my lectures muffled up to the ears.

The feeling that one had entered a prison was further enhanced by the sight of the students, with their closely shaven heads and dingy black uniforms. It is the custom in all Japanese schools for the boys to shave their heads, but until a few years ago the rule was not enforced in the case of university students. As the China war progressed, however, additional austerity became the rule and at the instigation of the army authorities all male students were required to shave their heads. Shaving the head was, however, interpreted as wearing the hair short enough to make a parting impossible, and the use of any form of oil or dressing unnecessary. In this matter, to sail as close to the wind as possible was, I noticed, the sign of a liberal mind. It always seemed curious to me that this military craze for shaving the head should not be applied to the face, and doubly strange in a people that prides itself on its cleanliness: a closely shaven head was often accompanied by a face that no razor had touched for five or six days.

The same professor who had welcomed me at Yokohama was my guide on this occasion of my first lecture, and ushered me into the class room. We entered in silence, the students rising to their feet and bowing from the waist. He took the only available chair on the dais, and left me to stand at his side feeling rather like a prisoner in the dock. After calling over the names of the students, he began what was apparently a brief description of my life history. I could not, of course, understand one word of what he was saying, except for the occasional interpolation of English words—Cambridge University, Mount Everest Expedition, and so on. He stopped as abruptly as he had started, bowed low and left me alone with the

EDUCATION

class. I managed somehow or other to struggle through my lecture, but without eliciting any response. It was like talking through a plate glass window; the students could obviously see me, but their fixed expressions almost persuaded me that they could not hear what I was saying. At the end I asked for questions, but no one raised his voice. They apparently understood, however, that the lesson was ended, for again they rose to their feet, once more bowed from the waist and filed silently out of the room. This was my first introduction to a Japanese public. I was later to learn that my students did possess individuality, although their whole education is conducive to its suppression. It was a very long time before I could get any student to express a personal opinion. Invariably they used the first person plural, and it was not until I became intimate with one or two of them that I obtained a key to the individual heart. There is a world of difference between the I of self and the we of the herd; but until the foreigner in Japan has learned to separate the two, he has not begun to understand the human side of the Japanese people.

It must have been a few days later that I was sitting at my desk in the common room when one of my Japanese colleagues crept silently up and without any preliminary opening started to whisper in my ear. "Last night," he murmured, "my house was burned to the ground and my wife and two children perished in the conflagration." I swung round on my chair and tried to find words appropriate to the occasion, but it became apparent that the calamity had not actually taken place. "I merely wish to know," he explained, "if the sentence which I spoke is formed in correct English."

For the first few weeks I felt exceedingly depressed. I was making absolutely no headway, for it had now become quite obvious that my class could hardly understand a word of what I said. It appeared to me that what was really required was not lectures on literature but lessons in English. I told the Professor this, but he would not agree, his opinion being that a certain number of incomprehensible lectures were salutary: they kept the students from overestimating their ability to understand spoken English. With this end in view, he himself invariably used one or other of the later works of Henry James as a text-book for teaching conversation, which possibly accounted for the fact that the students of this particular university were quite incapable of making a plain statement plainly. One day I noticed that one of the students had remained behind, apparently wishing to speak to me. I asked him what the matter was. "Sir," he said, "it is our earnest wish to inform you that we are not contempting you. We have been perusing a book in which it is stated that the smile is sometimes used as a contempt in England. In Japan this is not so. When we smile it is because we do not understand so well; we do not contempt." After some months my class began to thaw, but the ice was not really broken until one morning, when coming into the class room, I found the following notice written on the blackboard. " Sir," it said, " to-day we do not wish lecture on T. S. Eliot. We wish to practise hearing King's English and hope for intimate lecture on details of your love-life. Have you visited Japanese gay quarter?"

The outstanding merits of the Japanese educational system are that it is both cheap and democratic. There is none of the snobbery which is such a marked feature of our English educational system, the schools and universities being open to all without regard to wealth or class.

A sharp distinction is, however, made between government and private educational institutions. Nearly all schools up to the secondary grade are controlled by the government, the only exceptions being a few missionary and private foundations. To-day, however, the education provided in the latter does not differ from that given in the government schools. About ninety per cent of the youth of Japan receives its education, at any rate up to about the age of sixteen, in a government school.

Elementary schools are co-educational, but in all later stages of education the sexes are rigidly segregated. After completing his elementary course the boy moves on to a middle school, where he stays until the age of sixteen or so. After the middle school the road forks, for on completing this course he must decide whether or not he will aim at entering a university. To do so he must first graduate from one or other of the so-called high schools, a proceeding which takes a further three years. The Japanese High School is the nearest equivalent to the English Public School, but the education it provides is more advanced, being rather specialized. The High School course is in fact a preliminary university course. But it is not easy to enter a High School, for not only is the entrance examination extremely difficult, but of those who qualify, only about one in thirty secures admission owing to the lack of vacancies. In addition to a sound knowledge of national subjects such as Japanese history and the Chinese classics, a high standard in mathematics and the mastery of at least two foreign languages (one of which must be English) are required. The study of classical Chinese, it should be noted, is to a Japanese what Latin and Greek are to us.

In the entrance examination in 1941 the English paper called for the translation of a long passage out of *Sartor Resartus* into Japanese. The examiners have a predilection for Carlyle and Emerson, and one boy told me that in order to make sure of passing the

EDUCATION

examination he and his friends had compiled a list of all the unusual words of which Carlyle makes use, and had committed their meanings to memory. A favourite method, by the way, of committing words to memory is to carry about a number of small slips, each about the size of a visiting card. A Japanese word is written on one side with its English equivalent on the other, and in trams and buses one often sees students working through their piles of cards. I was once strap-hanging next to a boy who was thus engaged when my eye was caught by the extraordinary length of the word he was trying to memorize. I asked him to show me his card. The word was *floccinaucinihilipilification*. I asked him what it meant. He gave me a definition that had some connection with the theory of money, I forget exactly what, and then added, rather contemptuously, I thought, that every Japanese schoolboy knew it. "Because," he said, "it is the longest word in the English language." [1]

I used to give occasional lectures at the First High School in Tokyo, which has the reputation, and rightly I think, of being the best school of its kind in Japan. The Japanese have a passion for comparing everyone and everything in their country with someone or something in Europe. Thus we find the Japanese Alps, the Japanese Riviera, the Japanese Shakespeare, and so on. The First High School was sometimes referred to by its students as the Japanese Eton, that venerable institution being associated in their minds with the finest possible education. It would be hardly possible, however, to think of a more unsuitable comparison, for the majority of the boys came from extremely poor families. In only one way did the school resemble Eton; a very large proportion of those who attain to high government office have been educated there.

It is the custom in all High Schools to dress untidily, and the boys here took pride in wearing clothes that were little better than rags. One boy in my class was so infamously clad that I thought he must really be destitute, and I meditated buying him a decent suit of clothes. To my surprise, however, he called at my house one day with a very expensive camera, and on questioning one of his classmates I discovered that he was the son of a millionaire. This custom originated, I understand, in the desire to avoid any sign of distinction between the sons of the rich and the poor, and for a similar reason the food with which the boys are daily provided is of the

---

[1] For the benefit of the reader whose knowledge of the English language is as limited as my own, I should perhaps note that the *Concise Oxford Dictionary* gives the meaning of the word floccinaucinihilipilification as "estimating as worthless." "Full of Sound and Fury," one might almost say, but "signifying nothing."

EDUCATION

cheapest possible quality. Some of the boys come from such poor homes that their parents cannot afford to give them any pocket-money, and because of this nearly every First High School boy spends two or three evenings a week in acting as a tutor. The average middle school student is unable to pass the High School entrance examination without special assistance, and because the First High School has such a high reputation there is always a demand for the services of its students to act as tutors.

The boys live in dormitories in the school grounds and without any supervision, no member of the staff living anywhere near them. It is in fact an unwritten law that no master shall enter the dormitories except at the invitation of the students. My own house was quite near the school and I would often hear the boys returning to the dormitory as late as one o'clock in the morning; usually they were coming back from some beer-drinking party. But Japanese beer is an extremely innocuous beverage and many of the students had reached the age of twenty. Drinking and smoking were not encouraged, but they were not forbidden; nor were any particular restrictions placed on the boys' movements out of school hours. The system seemed to work well. Japanese boys are extremely docile, and I can state with confidence that the students of the First High School did not abuse their privileges.

Higher education is provided by the government in the Imperial Universities, the one at Tokyo being the largest and best. There are in all six Imperial Universities situated in Japan and one each in Korea and Formosa, the total number of students being about twenty-two thousand with a yearly graduation of some seven thousand. No one who has not taken his degree at one or other of the Imperial Universities can hope to be employed by the government, and most students do in fact take up some form of government work. A government post is every boy's ambition. It means security; not for him alone, but also for his parents, who, together with other relatives, are in many cases pinching and scraping in order to help him through his university years. For if a young man is freed from the necessity of earning his pocket money he can obviously pay more attention to his studies. In most countries in the world there is competition to secure government employment. In Japan it plays altogether too great a part. The system has much in common with that which obtained in ancient China, where a man's whole career depended upon his success in government examinations.

In addition to the Imperial Universities, higher government education is provided by a number of technical colleges, some of which are from time to time raised to university status. In this group

EDUCATION

there are schools of art, music, dentistry, and foreign languages, and several colleges which specialize in the training of teachers.

But there is such a demand for higher education in Japan that the government universities alone cannot meet it, and large numbers of private foundations have been given the official standing of a university. In Tokyo, for instance, there are no less than fifteen of these. In such places the education provided varies greatly; it is often far below the normal university standard, but in the best it is as good as, if not better than, that obtainable at the Imperial University. The two best known of the private universities are Waseda and Keio. It was to Keio that I got myself transferred when I could no longer stand the prison-like atmosphere of my first university. Keio, which was founded earlier than any of the government institutions, is the oldest university in Japan, and in my opinion the finest in the country. Its founder was a man of extremely liberal views, and it used to be known as "The English University," because most of the instruction there was formerly given in that language. It has, moreover, kept up its tradition for liberal-mindedness, perhaps because the majority of its professors and senior lecturers are men who have been educated abroad. Following a curriculum of its own, it is not looked upon with favour either by the Department of Education, the Police, or the Army. But this makes it less of a "forcing house" than any other university in Japan. Being a very rich foundation, it is not dependent upon government grants, and the majority of its graduates, since they are barred from government service, eventually go into business. Most of the industrial leaders of the country were educated at Keio. Many of these are millionaires, and consequently men of influence, and this makes it difficult for the government to interfere in the internal affairs of the university. There is as much competition to get into Keio as into the Imperial universities since its graduates are assured of obtaining good business appointments.

Of the remaining private universities little need be said except that to graduate at some of them is no great feat. But the Japanese place an exaggerated value on the possession of academic degrees. There seems to have been a time when the Department of Education was willing to raise the status of almost any large school or college to that of a university, and to-day the supply of graduates far exceeds the demand for recruits to the learned professions. But the Japanese university graduate, unlike his fellow in India, does not consider it beneath his dignity to enter trade or commerce. Bank clerks, for instance, are nearly always university graduates, and it is quite common to find shop assistants who have taken a degree in economics.

EDUCATION

The Japanese do, however, discriminate between degree and degree, and the type of appointment a graduate secures depends very largely upon the university from which he comes. It would not be difficult to criticize the system of education, but it must at least be said in fairness that higher education, such as it is in Japan, is probably more widespread than in any other country.

There are no residential universities in Japan; nor are the students in any way supervised. Most of them live in small one-roomed lodgings, in conditions of extreme discomfort. They take their meals in one or other of the thousands of little eating houses which swarm in the back streets of Tokyo, where for the equivalent of about sixpence one can obtain lunch or dinner of a sort. Study is done mostly in the university library. There is no contact between teacher and pupil; in fact the classes are so large in some faculties, law and economics for instance, that the teacher does not even know the names of his students. Instruction is impersonal; there is nothing that even faintly resembles our own tutorial system. Remembering how much I had learnt from my tutor in my own university days, and how little I had profited from lectures, I tried to change the Japanese system, but without success. In all departments the syllabus is so overloaded that my students merely looked upon the innovation as a heaven-sent opportunity to make up arrears in other subjects. Instead of coming to discuss their problems with me, they simply stayed away.

At the Imperial University the average expenses of a student are one hundred yen per month, roughly £6 10s. This includes fees, books and all living expenses, with a small margin for amusement. In some cases this sum is provided entirely out of government scholarships; but a student's total annual expenses are so low that there is hardly a family in Japan that cannot somehow or other raise the necessary sum. It may put considerable strain on a family that is really poor, but it should be remembered that to have a member of the family graduate at the Imperial University is in Japan a form of insurance, the rewards of which will later be enjoyed by all those who have pinched and scraped to provide it. The great evil of the system is the appalling responsibility placed upon the shoulders of young and growing men. At a time when they ought to be developing both mentally and physically they feel they already have a millstone round their necks; most of them cannot afford the luxury of education for its own sake. The system takes a terrible toll on the youth of the nation. There are unfortunately no published statistics, but a Japanese colleague of mine who was interested in the subject had for a number of years kept track of all the students who passed

EDUCATION

through his hands at the First High School, and of these one in ten had to give up through ill health before graduating from the Imperial University. The trouble was nearly always tuberculosis. There is a great deal of this disease in Japan, and complete recovery is rare. It is to be expected, too, that the incidence of tuberculosis will be considerably increased by the drastic shortening of school and university vacations, other wartime austerity measures (such as the non-heating of class rooms in winter), and the general lowering of the standard of living.

Military training is now compulsory in all Japanese schools and universities, including even the Academies of Art and Music. Every educational institution in the country has a number of army officers attached to it, the majority of them being on the active list. They are in theory subordinate to the principal of the school, but in actual practice have a great deal of power. The amount of time devoted to military instruction is supposed to be about five or six hours a week, but "special" periods of instruction are now often added, usually in the hours allotted to one or other of the foreign teachers, or at some time when the students would otherwise be studying what in the senior officer's opinion is some unnecessary subject, literature or philosophy, for instance. The military instruction includes lectures on discipline and the merit in dying for one's country. There is also a certain amount of field work, which includes route marches of anything up to twenty-five miles. I noticed that from some of these the boys returned completely exhausted. Once a year each class is required to undergo field training, lasting for about one week, and for this purpose the students are taken right away from the school and segregated in special barracks in the country, where they are under strict military discipline. During this period work starts before dawn and is continued until nightfall.

I have no hesitation in saying that military training is the most unpopular feature of Japanese school life. Every student I knew loathed it and would seize eagerly upon the slightest opportunity to avoid attendance. But at the present time the army controls everything in Japan and there is nothing anyone can do. Just before I left, somewhat half-hearted attempts were, it is true, being made to modify the army's interference with education; but in a country which is more or less totalitarian what can a mere school-master do when he finds himself up against the generals? The only interest the Japanese army has in education is to get it over as quickly as possible in order to swell the flow of recruits.

★ 11 ★

I USED TO GO ABOUT A GREAT DEAL WITH MY STUDENTS, AND AT FIRST hardly an evening passed when the house was not filled with them. These visits were at first a source of embarrassment. The Japanese set great store by ceremony and the avoidance of giving offence, but they seem incapable of understanding that well-bred people behave in much the same way all over the world. They have a fixed idea that the English or American code of manners is something different from their own. Rather than take the risk of appearing rude they would sit stiffly silent, perched on the edge of their chairs. Or if they spoke at all it would be to utter a few carefully-prepared phrases, the nature of which was invariably the same. What were my impressions of Japan? Why had I come and how long did I propose to stay? What did I think of Japanese women? And so on. I must have answered these and similar questions hundreds of times; they were not intended to be inquisitive, nor were my interrogators particularly interested in the replies I gave. It was simply that this was the traditional Japanese idea of how to converse with a foreigner. It must be remembered also that, as in ancient China, the profession of teaching is regarded with great respect in Japan. I, therefore, as a teacher and a foreigner called for a double dose of formality.

In course of time, however, I was able to make it clear that ceremony was odious to me, and that if they could bring themselves to put it aside and treat me as an ordinary human being I should be glad to see them whenever they cared to come. We would often talk far into the night; and it was chiefly as a result of these conversations that I came little by little to build up some idea of Japanese psychology.

I gradually discovered that there is a very great difference between the mentality of the young Japanese and that of older generations, and that this difference is not the one normally to be found in members of different age groups. I should say that it is due principally to the rapid pace with which the country has been modernized.

We are often told that Japanese regard themselves as the children of the gods and that they believe in the divinity of their Emperor. How far is this true? To be sure, the *Kojiki*, the ancient chronicle of Japan, ascribes a divine origin to the Emperor and hence to the people in general, since the Emperor is looked upon as the father of the nation, which is thought of as one huge family. But the *Kojiki* was written early in the eighth century, and no intelligent Japanese takes its mythology as literal truth. I should say that he looks upon it much as an intelligent Christian regards the Old Testament, as a mixture of fact and fancy.

Nevertheless the myth of divinity has played an exceedingly important part in the expansion of nationalist feeling, and the leaders of Japan have cleverly exploited it to gain their ends. It has been built up by methods similar to those employed by advertising agents, that is to say it has been constantly brought to the notice of the people. It is the method adopted by Dr. Goebbels for misleading the German people, also that employed by the manufacturers of soap and tooth paste, but the Japanese thought of it first. They do not necessarily believe it, but since they are never for one moment allowed to forget it there comes a time when all but the intelligent and sceptical tacitly accept the myth.

The outward signs by which the Emperor's divinity is proclaimed are many and various. No one may look down upon him from a higher level, as a result of which the police order the lowering of blinds of all upper windows in any street along which he is due to pass. When the present headquarters of the Metropolitan Police Board were built it was afterwards discovered that the tower overtopped the Imperial Palace, near which it stands, by several feet. The result was that the tower had to be removed, and the building now presents a strangely unfinished appearance. Whenever the Emperor has occasion to go by road from one place to another the streets on his route are cleared for a distance of about half a mile on either side, so that his motor passes through what must to him appear a completely deserted city. On the rare occasions when he appears in public, such as the annual military review or the periodical ceremonial visits to the various shrines, onlookers are supposed to avert their gaze as he passes, but in practice many doubtless manage to catch a glimpse. I remember on one occasion being stopped in a side street for nearly an hour. It was not possible even to see into the main road along which His Imperial Highness was due to pass and, in spite of the fact that it was a bitterly cold winter's day, the police, of whom there are always thousands on duty on every such occasion, made us remove our overcoats as a remark of respect. In criticizing matters of this sort it is well, however, not to lose one's sense of proportion; we ourselves have the custom of uncovering when the King's colour passes. The difference is that in Japan the ceremonial aspect of the matter has been distorted and given a grossly exaggerated form.

Every school and university in Japan has a photograph of the Emperor, and in a fire or any other calamity this portrait must at all costs be saved. There are cases on record when a school principal has lost his life in attempting to save the Imperial photograph; or, having failed in his attempt, has committed suicide. Perhaps a schoolmaster would hardly go to quite such lengths at the present day, but there is no doubt that should the Emperor's photograph suffer destruction in his school he would certainly be called upon to resign. In order to guard against this possibility, photographs are nowadays kept in a fire-proof structure, specially erected for that purpose at some distance from the main building. On all ceremonial occasions the Imperial photograph is displayed in schools, and at such times both staff and pupils pay homage to it in exactly the same way as they would were the Emperor actually present.

The young Japanese of the educated classes is not as a rule unduly nationalistic, and certainly does not believe in the divinity of the Emperor, or his own descent from the gods. My pupils would talk quite frankly on these subjects and never made any attempt to disguise their dislike of the actual trend of affairs. Communism was growing among this class until a few years ago when the police endeavoured to stamp it out by arresting all those who were known to incline to "dangerous thought." Many thousands of young men are still in gaol to-day, and it is unlikely that any leaders of the movement are still at large. Nevertheless, I believe it would be a mistake to suppose that the communist movement no longer exists in Japan.

Among the students personally known to me, two committed suicide by throwing themselves in front of trains on the eve of their being called to the army. Their friends afterwards explained to me that their motive was not unwillingness to undergo military training, as such, but an overwhelming belief that the army's domination of their country was not in Japan's best interests. In the Japan of to-day the unorthodox can prove the courage of their convictions only by suicide.

It would be possible, I think, to divide the Japanese into three distinct classes, each of which represents not only an age group but also a point of view. There is, first of all, the group which comprises most of the youth of the country up to the age of twenty-five or so. The outstanding characteristic of this group is mental confusion. As one of my own students put it: " we are all of us now ' sicklied o'er with the pale cast of thought.' " It should be remembered that the boys of this generation received their first education at a time when liberal thought was still comparatively popular in Japan. The higher education they are at present undergoing is based entirely on Occidental ideas, and the more intelligent of them see quite clearly that there is no real hope for their country until such time as it assimilates not only the material benefits which the Western world has to offer, but also our philosophical and social ideas. In this connection it should, however, be realized that in the past few years elementary education in Japan has become extremely nationalistic, and subsequent classes of students are likely to be very different psychologically from those of the present generation. It is, in fact, not unlikely that their " re-education " may later present as great a problem as will undoubtedly arise in post-war Germany.

The second group comprises all the men between roughly the ages of twenty-five and forty-five. Contained in this group are most of the violent reactionaries. Many of them have received a Western education and are nationalistic almost to the point of insanity : they understand the necessity for a close study of the West, but only as a means of destroying it. I was always amazed at the speed and suddenness with which the first group changed to the second after entering upon a career. It was as striking as is the psychological change that takes place in the young men of more primitive communities who have to undergo an initiation ceremony. I suppose the reason is to a great extent economic. When it is a question of earning one's daily bread one comes up against the disadvantage of holding views diametrically opposed to those of the majority. The youth of Japan is not alone in coming under such pressure, but in no other country, excepting perhaps Germany, is the pressure so ruthlessly applied.

After the middle forties another very striking change is to be found. There is a tendency to ignore foreign ideas altogether, and to return to the traditional Japanese way of living. The men of this group are not, generally speaking, particularly anti-foreign; it is simply that they seem to give up the struggle. Business men, and others who for years have lived a more or less Westernized life, change completely. They take to the kimono, cease to eat foreign food, and spend their leisure in following purely Japanese pursuits ; the practice of calligraphy, the study of Japanese art and literature, and so on. Many of these middle-aged men have been long accustomed to the foreign style of living and have built themselves houses which are a compromise between the West and the East. This reversion to the traditional way of life comes gradually. It is complete when a father hands his Tokyo house over to his children and retires to a villa in the country. Some of my students used to take me to visit their parents who had thus retired. These country houses were noticeably free from Occidental trappings and elegant in the old Japanese style.

This last change which comes over the Japanese is in some ways comparable with that which comes over many English people who, as they approach old age, start to take an almost morbid interest in religion.

It should be noted, however, that at no time does the father relax his hold over his children: in fact, as he becomes older he expects to be obeyed even more implicitly.

To the wonder of the European, retired generals sometimes become Buddhist priests and spend their declining years officiating in some lonely temple. This is merely another manifestation of the return to a Japanese way of living. One well-known general, who distinguished himself in the China campaign, became a priest shortly before I left Japan, and his action was given prominence in the press as evidence of the spirituality of the Japanese army. In an interview which he gave shortly before entering the priesthood he explained that he was haunted by the fact that he had been responsible for the death in battle of many of his men, and that he was becoming a priest in order to devote the rest of his life to praying for the repose of their souls.

★ *12* ★

THE STUDENTS WITH WHOM I CAME IN CONTACT WERE, I SHOULD SAY, fairly representative of the educated youth of the country, and as I got to know them I was forced to change my ideas about the Japanese character. They surprised me by their sensitiveness, their sensibility, and the range of their interests, which was often remarkably wide. I found in most of them an overwhelming desire really to understand Western thought. They were well aware of the deficiencies of their own educational system, and would often describe it as a sort of factory for the mass production of bureaucrats, a very just assessment. Nearly all had a great desire to complete their studies either in England or America. They were convinced that the teaching of science, medicine, and engineering in Japan was inferior to European or American teaching, and in my opinion they were right. In only one branch of science have the Japanese proved themselves pre-eminent; since early times they have possessed a wide knowledge of botany and their contributions in this particular field have been notable.

The Japanese are often accused of being bad linguists, and they themselves often speak of this as a national disability which nothing can remedy. I was struck by the fact that many Japanese of the older generation, men now in the fifties and sixties, spoke English, or whatever their second language happened to be, markedly better than their juniors. Their vocabulary might be limited; but they handled their words easily, whereas the younger men, while they could read almost anything, were for the most part quite unable to express even a simple request in any spoken language other than their own. The reasons for this are worth considering in detail because they do something to explain the gradual decline of the Japanese standards in other fields, medicine, engineering, science, and even art.

At the time of the Meiji restoration, in 1868, the government of Japan was largely in the hands of men who had received their education abroad. These men, more far-seeing than the general run of their countrymen, had escaped to foreign parts at a time when it was actually a penal offence to quit the country.

As the leaders of Japan in the later days of the nineteenth century, they saw very clearly that their nation would never be able to compete with other nations until it had a comparable system of education. This was at the time of Britain's greatest expansion, and it was natural that a study of the English language should form an important part of the new programme. The teaching of English was at first largely in the hands of missionaries. Some of the best universities in Japan started as small missionary schools, and remained under foreign control until December, 1941, when the government took drastic action. Until comparatively recently, then, classes were small and a certain amount of individual instruction was given. Moreover, the language was taught by a teacher whose mother-tongue it was. With the country's rapid industrialization the need for instruction in foreign languages quickly increased, and the study of English has for many years been compulsory in all Japanese schools. The average schoolboy often now devotes about five hours a week to English, and the number of hours is considerably increased after the age of sixteen by those boys who intend eventually to enter a university. It can be said that most educated Japanese have spent some thousands of hours in the study of English, and yet at the end of this time many of them are quite unable to frame the simplest sentence correctly. This is to be explained by the lack of foreign teachers. It is obvious that the many thousands of teachers required could not be recruited from abroad; the expense alone would prohibit it. But there is a tendency in Japan to dispense with foreign help at the earliest possible moment; and since the study of English was early introduced it was only natural that this should have been one of the first subjects to be " Japanized."

Until December, 1941, there were still a number of English and American teachers, but these were all specially employed, either to train Japanese who would in due course themselves become teachers of English, or (as in my own case) to lecture on English literature to university students who in theory were supposed to know the actual language before matriculating.

The man who is unable to speak the foreign language he is by way of teaching naturally does not wish to expose his ignorance to his pupils. It follows, therefore, that English instruction in present-day Japan is almost entirely through the written word, usually by means of word-for-word translation from one language into the other. It is by no means uncommon for a Japanese teacher of English never to have heard the language spoken by a native. Little wonder, then, that the students should find an English lecturer at first incomprehensible. I have stressed this point because the same state of affairs is found in nearly every other department of Japanese life, and with the same eventual loss of efficiency. In medicine, engineering, in general science, in anything you like, the story is the same. The Japanese who has been trained abroad is nearly always proficient, and at the time of return to his native country has little if anything more to learn. But he does not keep up with the times; he grows rusty. This may be due to the fact that in Japan itself there is so little stimulation, so little contact with the research that is being carried on in the outside world; or it may be, as Westerners have often suggested, that the Japanese, while extremely skilful at copying, lack creative power. They themselves deny this and claim that their particular genius lies in improving foreign culture and adapting it to their own peculiar needs.

Occidental forms of painting have been for many years extremely popular in Japan, and there was a time not so long ago when excellent work was being produced by artists trained for the most part in Paris. But Japan now has schools of its own in which Western art is taught. Western art, like the English language, is in Japanese official opinion something that has now been mastered. The fruits of this home teaching may be seen in the frequent exhibitions in Tokyo. They are for the most part lamentable, and as time goes on the standard will deteriorate still further.

The story is more or less the same in nearly every other field. Take, for instance, aviation. The Navy " Zero " is said at present to be Japan's best fighter and is believed to have been designed in Germany. But it has been " adapted " and " improved " by the Japanese to such an extent that the pilot has practically no protection. The only reason why it has hitherto been so successful is because the Japanese possessed so many; we were unable to compete against their superior numbers. But already, in the operations in New

Guinea, the "Zero" has proved no match for the most modern American fighters. The extremely large Japanese Air Force is something we cannot afford to disregard, but we do not need to fear that they can outstrip us in designing.

Japan's desire to emancipate herself from foreign influence is, of course, no new thing. The movement has been growing steadily for many years, but it did not really come to a head until the outbreak of war. It took the form at first of a violent press campaign against the teaching of English and advocated its complete abolition. This has always been one of the favourite stalking horses of the extreme reactionaries, but it cannot be said to have had many supporters. Most Japanese are at any rate realists, and understand perfectly well that a certain knowledge of the English language is an absolute necessity, if only for the purpose of carrying on foreign trade. But on this occasion the clamour became so insistent that it was only silenced when the Prime Minister, General Tojo, replying to a speech in the Diet, pointed out that while sympathizing with the patriotic motives that prompted the desire to abolish the study of an enemy language, it was in his opinion necessary not to do away with English instruction but even to increase the number of hours devoted to it. "We shall require," he said, "large numbers of English speakers to administer our conquered territories. In Australia alone the figure will be enormous." He concluded his speech by saying that it would be many years before the people of those territories could acquire a sufficient knowledge of Japanese to make the use of English no longer necessary.

★ *13* ★

BEFORE THE WAR, THERE WERE IN TOKYO ALONE SOME TWO HUNDRED daily newspapers, which varied as much in their political and general outlook as do papers in any other country. Of these the best is still the *Asahi*, which is Japan's counterpart of *The Times*. Like any other great national newspaper, it had its own correspondents stationed all over the world, and used to be noted for the accuracy of its news and its reasoned judgment. At the other end of the scale were papers like the *Hochi*, which specialized in scandal. It should be noted in this connection that in Japan there is no law of libel, so that the private life and idiosyncrasies of prominent individuals, and particularly of politicians, have always been at the mercy of the scurrilous, especially at election times. But there are, of course, limits to what may be said with impunity, and many of the papers which specialized in sailing close to the wind kept themselves prepared for trouble by having two editors, a real one, whose name was never published and was unknown except to very few, and another who publicly occupied the chair, and when necessary went to prison. Scurrility was pushed so far at one time that it was not unusual for a newspaper to have several of its "editors" in gaol at the same time. But all this has now changed. The government now exercises a strict control over everything that is printed, and many papers have been forced to amalgamate. Moreover, as there is now only one political party in Japan the surviving newspapers no longer reflect different shades of opinion. Indeed they are all very much alike. Although they subscribe to the well-known foreign agencies, they have little use for the information they obtain, being obliged to print what they receive from *Domei*, the Japanese government agency, which has its own correspondents in all parts of the world. And even this news is, of course, severely censored before it is issued to the press. Previous to Japan's entry into the war, official news from German and Italian sources was given great prominence in the Japanese press, but this ceased almost immediately after Pearl Harbour. As a journalist friend told me : "We have now a war of our own ; we are no longer interested in what happens in Europe." It was the same man, at heart no friend of the Axis, who told me that the Italian Embassy was constantly complaining that so little space was given to the doings of their compatriots. Things came to such a pass that the Italian Press Attaché was finally moved to make an official protest. At the time he made his visit my friend happened to have on his table a pile of cables from foreign countries, all of them dealing with Italian reverses. "Look," he said, pointing to the pile, "these all concern your country. If you really wish it I will obtain permission to have them published."

But the most frequent complaints came from the German Embassy and these throw an interesting sidelight on Nazi methods. It appears that Berlin subscribes to all the more important Japanese papers and makes a daily analysis of any information concerning Germany. If the Japanese comment is in any way displeasing to the *Reich* it immediately cables to Tokyo asking if the Embassy has lodged a complaint ; and if not, why ? Thus, in order to retain their positions, Nazi officials in Tokyo are forced to keep up a more or less constant bombardment of the Japanese press. One editor told me that dealing with complaints from the German Embassy had become a regular part of his daily work; not a day passed but he received at least one. Before the war, the Propaganda Ministry in Berlin was chiefly concerned with reports on the British war effort. It wanted these to be suppressed, or at least severely " edited." The Japanese press did what it could to comply, but until Pearl Harbour there was a limit to the lengths it was prepared to go in falsifying the news.

In addition to the vernacular press, Tokyo has several dailies printed in English, but none in any other foreign language. These were at one time owned and run entirely by foreigners. Americans for the most part. The best known of them, *The Japan Advertiser*, built up for itself an enviable reputation for the reliability and impartiality of its news; and because it often contained information that appeared in no other paper its circulation was by no means confined to the foreigners in Tokyo. It has been the training ground for many journalists who have specialized in Far Eastern affairs and now enjoy world fame. The best known of these is probably Hugh Byas, who edited the paper for a number of years and later became correspondent in Japan for both the London and New York *Times* until he retired in 1940. There is probably no foreigner now living who knows so much about the intricacies of Japanese politics as he does. He was succeeded as *The Times* correspondent by Otto Tolischus, who arrived in Japan shortly after the publication of a book in which he described his experiences in Berlin. As the author of *They Wanted War*, he naturally did not meet with a very warm welcome from his Nazi colleagues.

As early as 1938 the freedom of foreign newspapermen in Japan was already becoming restricted; and the difficulties of running a newspaper rapidly became so great that the game was no longer worth the candle. *The Japan Advertiser* was the first paper to come on the market and was immediately bought by the Foreign Office. The majority of its staff continued to work under the new management, and there was not at first any marked difference in its tone. By degrees, however, the foreign staff either resigned or were discharged, and presently the Foreign Office chose a new editor. After this, it soon became nothing more nor less than a vehicle for government propaganda, and from a purely news point of view it was less informative even than the controlled vernacular press. Nevertheless, the translated extracts from the Japanese press, of which it published a daily column, sometimes made it amusing reading. Here are two extracts which illustrate the working of the divided Japanese mind.

" *The Nichiro Gyogyo Kaisha*, which kills for canning purposes large numbers of salmon every year, held its annual ceremony in the Company Board Rooms at 11 a.m. Thursday for the repose of the souls of the salmon. Following the ceremony, the Staff of the company was given a holiday for the rest of the day."—*From the issue dated 3rd October, 1941.*

" An artificial eye factory owned by Mr. Kakekichi Komagata of Mishima village, Shizuoka Prefecture, is now busily engaged in making a giant glass eye which will be offered to the Kanno Temple at Asakusa to console soldiers who have lost their sight in the China affair. The work will be finished about two months later."—*From the issue dated 4th April, 1941.*

The other papers in English were soon squeezed out of circulation. This was done by cutting down their supplies of paper so drastically that it became impossible for them to carry on. The Foreign Office bought them all, and then amalgamated them.

The only paper that held out right to the end was *Japan News-Week*. This American owned and edited paper was started as late as 1938, but its proprietor, W. R. Wills, had been in Japan for many years and had numerous friends in high places. It had as its policy the furtherance of American-Japanese relations, but it also contrived to publish a good deal of British news that appeared in no other paper. It was remarkable chiefly for the frankness of its leading articles, which were as critical of American as of Japanese foreign policy. In more normal times it might have done considerable good, since its policy was warmly supported by most of the big Japanese business houses, many of which continued to advertise in it until they were officially ordered to cease. As the political situation deteriorated, however, the task of the editor became increasingly difficult and Wills soon became accustomed to finding a member of the Metropolitan Police Board waiting for him when he arrived at his office on Mondays. He, however, had his own methods of getting their objections overruled; and the police, having done their duty by lodging an official complaint, would retire satisfied.

I used to do a weekly column for this paper, usually in the form of a review of current literature. As the war progressed, however, I used it almost entirely for anti-German propaganda, thinly disguised in the form of a book review. The German Embassy used to complain periodically, but it was not until I referred to the Nazi system as an " evil cancer " that they took up the matter with the Foreign Office. The situation was certainly odd and could probably have arisen in no other country. I was after all an official of the Foreign Office, and yet I was writing articles in denunciation of Japan's closest ally. The Germans were justified in complaining. My immediate chief said so, but added that so far as the Foreign Office was concerned I could say anything I liked. After this there was no further interference, but henceforth I used to receive a weekly parcel of literature, " with the compliments of the German Embassy," designed to make me alter my views. It usually consisted of extracts from English books and papers which, divorced from their context, gave the impression that the writer was exposing brutalities in British colonial administration. A great many of the examples given were concerned with the British treatment of the Boers at the time of the South African War (admittedly not one of the brightest episodes in our history), and our refusal to grant independence to Ireland. Later on I learned that my name had been added to the Gestapo official " Black List."

★ *14* ★

THE JAPANESE ARE OMNIVOROUS READERS, PARTICULARLY OF MAGAzines, the circulation of which is probably higher than in any other country in the world. At one end of the scale are several ultraliterary monthlies; at the other a score of weeklies designed to appeal to women of the middle and lower classes. A great many regular magazine readers, however, never buy magazines, preferring to read them for nothing. It is a very common sight to find people thus engaged. Nearly every newsagent's shop in Tokyo is crowded all day long with people awaiting their turn. The Japanese, when they buy a magazine, do not seem to mind if it is dirty and almost falling to pieces as a result of having already been read by some twenty or thirty people. A great many of the articles are lifted straight out of British or American publications, and translated into Japanese. Credit is seldom given to the author; in fact a common practice among translators is to alter the articles slightly and publish them under their own names.

There is a great demand for every kind of foreign literature, particularly for the latest best-selling novels, translations of which often appear within two or three weeks of the first arrival of the original. The delicate questions of paying the foreign author and publisher, or even of obtaining permission to undertake translation, do not arise, as there is no law of copyright in Japan. The work of translation is expedited by tearing the foreign book into pieces and giving each separate bit to a different translator. The finished translation is often published as the work of some comparatively well known literary man, who allows his name to be used in return for a substantial consideration. Work of this nature is often undertaken by university students in the literary faculties in order to support themselves. One of my own students used to earn a regular income in this way, and on one occasion he showed me what he was doing. He had been given some thirty pages of an American novel to translate; there was no clue to its title, and his particular section started in the middle of one sentence and ended in the middle of another. It sometimes happens that two different translations of the same book appear on the market at more or less the same time, and it is for this reason that speed in translating has come to be of more importance than accuracy.

But I must not give a wrong impression of the position of foreign literature in Japan. There are plenty of highly-skilled translators who would never think of stooping to work of this nature. Nearly all the classics have been admirably translated, and there is a group of writers (the majority of them university professors) which specializes in producing the best modern books in excellent Japanese. But they are apt sometimes to be a little over ambitious. There are, for instance, two completely different translations of James Joyce's *Ulysses* which, I am told, bear no resemblance to each other or to the original.

In spite of all these translations the demand for books in foreign languages (and particularly in English) is also very great. But these, too, are often published without any reference to the owners of the copyright, the most flagrant example being a series bound in such a way as to look almost identical with the American " Modern Library " editions. The Japanese take the attitude that an author should feel sufficiently rewarded by the publicity he gains by having his works published in their country. No Japanese writer earns very much from the sale of his books, and they cannot understand that Somerset Maugham, H. G. Wells, and Bernard Shaw, to take three obvious instances, are rich not because they happen to be good writers, but because all three happen also to be exceptionally able business men. When the last-named visited Japan some years ago he was conducted round the library of the Tokyo Imperial University and shown with pride the shelves containing the various editions of his works that had been published in Japan; but his guides were quite unable to appreciate his point of view when, with his usual sardonic humour, he said that he wondered who had given permission for the work to be carried out, and who was drawing the royalties.

LITERATURE IN JAPAN

The Japanese engaged in the teaching of English have a great partiality for the works of Meredith, Henry James, Carlyle, Emerson and certain lesser writers of this period. One reason for this is that these authors were widely read at the time when the older generation of Japanese were studying in England. These latter now occupy nearly all the higher posts in the teaching profession, and it is only natural that their opinions should carry great weight. They have, to some extent, established the belief that the cream of modern Anglo-American thought is contained in the writings of this group of authors; and obviously it would be tactless, to say the least of it, for their juniors to disagree with them. Besides, the average Japanese who goes abroad to study often fails to keep up with the outside world on his return. His knowledge of colloquial English soon falls out of date and is inadequate for the proper understanding of a modern novel. To save trouble (and also to save his face) he goes on teaching from the same old books year after year. The foreign teacher in a Japanese school or university has to spend a great deal of time in priming his Japanese colleagues. The reader will perhaps remember my story of the burning house.

As for the students themselves, they do not accept the position willingly. Those who are making a special study of English literature are inclined to react by avoiding everything except the ultra modern, and consider writers earlier than Aldous Huxley, D. H. Lawrence or Ernest Hemingway out of date. There is a great interest in all forms of modern poetry, particularly for that of T. S. Eliot. The Japanese would, of course, inevitably have discovered Eliot in due course; but they have a great fondness for linking names together, and T. S. Eliot is inextricably associated in the Japanese mind with my predecessor, William Empson, by whom they were introduced to the former's work. There is not yet, so far as I am aware, a Japanese William Empson, but a Japanese T. S. Eliot will undoubtedly arise before many more years have passed.

The war did not, as one might have expected, make much difference to the number of students entering the English literature faculty; the proportion remained the same. Nor did the number of students who took up German markedly increase. But certain difficulties have arisen. The importation of English books dwindled and has now stopped, so that the Japanese student is now completely ignorant of what is happening in the literary world outside Japan. Moreover, the police have placed a ban on certain authors. Aldous Huxley's complete works, for instance, are on the Index since they are considered to encourage sexual promiscuity. Hardy has been let off rather more lightly, for so far *Tess* alone has incurred official displeasure. The black list of authors could be extended almost indefinitely, and this interference by the police has already had a paralysing effect upon the study of English literature. No teacher dare take the risk of using as a text-book anything that might be added to the Index. The police, too, have withdrawn many books from circulation by buying up all the available copies, both new and second-hand. Nor is this wholly a wartime innovation. The Japanese police have always taken an interest in the students' taste in literature, and when they came across *Das Kapital* some ten years ago they proscribed it at once and redoubled their vigilance.

Their procedure, however, remains haphazard. For instance, Sherriff's famous anti-war play *Journey's End* was still being used as a text-book as late as 1941. Generally speaking, however, anti-war books are completely taboo, as also are those which are regarded as leaning towards any form of liberal thought. Not less disliked, moreover, are books which suggest that the individual has a right to think for himself or have a personal life of his own. In a word, the democratic ideal is anathema to Japanese officialdom, which requires that the individual subordinate himself absolutely to the State. The people are taught to regard themselves as nothing more than potential fathers and mothers whose duty it is to provide recruits for the army, which in its turn exists for the greater glorification of the Empire. Is it not remarkable, then, that in spite of these conditions the principle of personal freedom appeals to the younger generation more than any other Western idea? On the rare occasions when they do oppose their families (it is usually in connection with marriage or the choice of a profession), they are inclined to go to an extreme, failing completely to realize that even in a society organized on democratic lines a certain amount of compromise is nearly always necessary.

The Japanese are taught not to display the emotions in any way whatsoever, and it is easy to understand why novels that deal frankly with the subject of love are now regarded with particular displeasure; not, of course, by the younger generation, but by those officially responsible for guiding the thought of the nation. It does not, of course, follow that many of the books now officially proscribed are not studied with avidity outside the class-room.

Before leaving the subject of foreign literature I should perhaps add that all books entering the country are censored before booksellers or individuals are allowed to take possession of them. Except in the case of certain authors, however, it is seldom that books are banned completely. What usually happens is that offending pages are removed by the censorship authorities and the books are then placed on sale in a mutilated form. In the case of books and papers addressed to individual foreign residents the censorship takes the form of removing all references to Japan which conflict with the official viewpoint. My own copy of Auden and Isherwood's *Journey to a War* reached me minus a photograph of a Japanese prisoner captured by the Chinese army, for it destroyed the legend that no Japanese soldier ever permits himself to be captured. Similarly, a copy of Pearl Buck's novel, *The Patriot*, was deprived of the few pages in which a young Japanese pacifist is described as committing suicide rather than allow himself to be conscripted.

★ *15* ★

I HAD NOW SPENT AN AUTUMN AND WINTER IN JAPAN. I HAD SEEN THE famous chrysanthemums, which attain to a splendour undreamed of in other countries, and was eagerly awaiting the arrival of the cherry blossoms. I must confess at once that they were something of a disappointment. It has since occurred to me that one of the chief beauties of trees lies in the movement of their leaves; in watching the emerald tracery weave patterns against the sky. But the cherries blossom before their leaves appear, and when seen in large masses they give the appearance of being artificial; they look like stage decor. The really exciting thing about the cherry blossom season is the suddenness with which it opens. One day there is apparently nothing but leaf buds, the next the trees are in full bloom. A week later, at the most, all is over, and the display is finished for another year.

The cherry is to the Japanese what the rose is to the English. It is the subject of innumerable poems, and every year vast crowds make excursions to the more famous plantations. The cherry is said to typify the Japanese view of life. It is a blaze of glory while it lasts; but its life is short. It does not fade gradually; its end is sudden, like that of a soldier killed in battle. It inspires a gaiety that is tinged with sadness, the sentiment dominant in the Japanese character.

But now I wished to see something of the country, and since the summer vacation was soon to begin I made plans to visit the mountains, taking with me one of my students. We decided to go to the Japanese Alps in order to escape the heat of the low lands, which are unbearable in summer.

Having no mountains of this altitude in England, we are inclined to regard Alpine climbing as a sport for the privileged minority; but in Japan the situation is quite different. Mountaineering has become one of the most popular of all sports, and its devotees range from Prince Chichibu, the brother of the Emperor, to the sturdy sons of farmers born and bred among Japan's numerous mountains. Moreover, the climbing grounds are so easy to reach that after leaving school or office on a Saturday afternoon one can be in the heart of the mountains by the late evening, spend the whole of Sunday climbing, and be back in Tokyo in time to start work again on Monday morning.

In no country is mountaineering more popular or better arranged than in Japan. Every university has its club, and in most of the climbing centres there are well appointed huts which are crowded with students throughout the year, for most of the mountains afford good ski-ing in winter.

The Japanese Alps are situated in the volcanic ranges extending through the central and widest part of the main island. This name, which is now in universal use, was first applied to the district by a Mr. William Gowland, an English engineer who was connected with the Osaka mint about fifty years ago. It was popularized by the late Rev. Walter Weston, one of the pioneers of climbing in Japan, in memory of whom the Japanese Alpine Club has recently affixed a plaque to the rocks in one of the most popular centres.

A large portion of the Alps has now been made a National Park. Fortunately, the prohibition with regard to picking wild flowers is scrupulously regarded; there is no wanton despoliation such as has, to a great extent, denuded Europe of some of its rarer plants. The Japanese are content only to admire and pass on. But they have not yet become "litter conscious," and the better-known tracks are strewn with the remains of meals, empty tins and discarded wrappings of every kind.

Most of the climbing in these Alps is easy. A European of average competence could tackle any of the peaks without risk. Yet fatal accidents are fairly numerous, the reasons for which are worth consideration.

It should be noted that the European technique of mountain climbing has been evolved on a basis of "safety first," although it must be admitted that between the wars a school of younger climbers which saw fit to disregard this principle came into being. Most of them were German. By taking the most unjustifiable risks they sought to enhance their national prestige by establishing world records, giving little thought to the safety of those who were often called upon to rescue them. There is a tendency in Japan, also, to indulge in this futile competition.

MOUNTAINEERING

The Japanese mountains are annually visited by thousands of people who have never climbed before, who know nothing about map reading, and are quite unprepared for the idiosyncracies of mountain weather. They have, in short, no mountain sense. As long as they stick to the beaten tracks they are perfectly safe; but many of them aspire to tackle difficulties which are quite beyond their powers. They get half-way up some mountain, and then, confronted by an unexpected difficulty, find themselves unable either to advance or retreat; or, mountain weather being notoriously changeable, they lose their way in the swirling mists and are benighted. During the summer of 1939 I happened to see in a Japanese newspaper a picture of a small child whose only claim to fame was that he was the youngest climber ever to make the ascent of Mount Yari. It so happens that my companion and I were on the top of this very mountain when this infant prodigy arrived. The baby, for he could not have been more than seven or eight years old, was clinging fearfully to his elder companion's neck, and I expected at every moment to see the pair go hurtling down the rocks. For this sort of thing there is absolutely no justification; the most likely result is that the child has acquired a morbid dread of heights from which it may possibly never recover.

In Europe and America, mountaineering seems to attract only the more intellectual lovers of physical exercise, but, as I have already pointed out, in Japan it is universally popular. For this there is, I think, a definite explanation. Appreciation of the beauties of nature and art is the heritage of the whole Japanese people (possibly their greatest heritage), and nowhere can nature be so well appreciated as in the mountains. Moreover, the Japanese of to-day are probably more addicted to physical exercise than any nation in the world. It is only natural, then, that any sport which could be combined with æsthetic pleasure was bound to make a strong appeal to them.

I was often asked what I thought of Japan's chances of success in the field of mountain exploration, a branch of the sport which they took up rather late. There has been only one Japanese expedition to the Himalayas, when a party of climbers, mostly university students, made the first ascent of Nanda Kot a few years ago. This peak, judged by Himalayan standards, is neither very difficult nor very high. It had, however, resisted several previous assaults, and the fact that it fell to the Japanese climbers at their first attempt is an index of their capability.

The Japanese as a race are short in stature, and the athletic type is lightly built. Both of these are useful qualities, for it has now been proved that the heavily built and very muscular type, the typical old style "athlete" is quite unsuited to high mountaineering. The Japanese, moreover, are one of the most disciplined races on earth and able to keep their individuality in check. This is likely to be one of their greatest assets, for the highest mountains in the world can only be conquered by the combined efforts of many people; there is no room for the brilliant individualist on such expeditions. However great a performer he may be, it is quite certain that unless he is able to suppress his personality and use his skill for the common good he will never conquer the greatest summits.

Owing to the widespread popularity of the sport, the Japanese are fortunate in possessing large numbers of highly skilled climbers, so that in organizing a big expedition they would have a large field from which to choose. The one thing they lack is mountains high enough to prove of value for training purposes, for the Japanese Alps are so low that difficulties in connection with altitude, one of the main bugbears of Himalayan exploration, do not arise. As for me, however, since my days in the big mountains belong definitely to the past, that was their greatest charm.

I liked the mountains best in winter. But except in the northern island of Hokkaido, where it is possible to enjoy some of the finest ski-ing in the world, the snow is not of the finest quality. This is because most of the more accessible ski-ing grounds are situated in the mountains near the sea, either the Pacific or the Japan Sea, so that the snow is often wet and sticky; only very seldom does one find it in that powdery condition which makes ski-ing in Switzerland so enjoyable. But even so, ski-ing in Japan is very popular among the younger generation and becoming more so year by year.

The Japanese mountains are of volcanic origin, and hot springs are numerous in the mountain resorts. Nothing is more enjoyable than the unique pleasure of finishing a hard day's ski-ing with a swim in an open-air pool so hot that the surrounding frozen air causes clouds of steam to rise. These springs, of which there are at least several thousand, are one of the most pleasant features of the countryside. I used to go regularly every Saturday to one or other of these resorts throughout the winter, but the most enjoyable time of all was in the Spring. Even as late as April there is still plenty of snow, and since by that time the sun's rays have become strong again most people find it possible to ski wearing practically no clothing. It was my habit to go off for a day in the mountains wearing nothing but boots and a pair of shorts, but one needs to be a hardened sun-bather before this is possible without becoming badly blistered.

The appearance of Mount Fuji is familiar all over the world; it is pictured on nearly every Japanese poster, advertisement and tourist

MOUNTAINEERING

booklet, and no play or film dealing with Japanese life is considered complete in which some aspect or other of it does not appear. It is, I should imagine, the best advertised mountain in the world. In spite of this, however, it does not give one the feeling, as do the better known of the Swiss Alps, that it has become self-conscious through being looked at too much. It is one of the very few famous " sights," like the New York skyscrapers, that really comes up to expectations. The mountain is visible from many parts of Tokyo, especially in the clear winter air, but it is seen at its best from the sea at dawn. At such times it seems to tower over everything, its perfect snow-capped cone, a purplish green in the light of early morning, seeming to be suspended in the sky. The beauty of Fuji is due to the simplicity of its outlines and the fact that it stands alone; from wherever one views it there is little else to distract the eye.

Mount Fuji, as everybody knows, is the highest mountain in Japan, rising 3,773 metres above the sea. I suppose this figure must appear in practically every geography and book of statistics published throughout the world; yet one of the first acts the government ordered after the outbreak of war was to forbid the printing of this information on postcards, maps, and so on.

The ascent of the mountain does not call for even the most elementary skill in mountaineering. There is a path, rough it is true, right to the summit, up which it would be possible to ride a motor cycle, while to a horseman the journey would not present the slightest difficulty. The road, however, is littered with advertisements, broken bottles, the remains of food and human excreta; and at every stage the weary traveller is importuned by begging priests who spend the summer months in the various shrines situated on the mountain's slopes. I made the pilgrimage with a party of my students, and we spent the afternoon and evening of a broiling August day toiling upwards over the gritty lava of which the mountain is composed. We slept the night at a hut about three-quarters of the way up and arrived on the summit, in company with several thousand other people, shortly before dawn. The view from the top was astounding: over a maze of still, dark lakes and valleys we looked out right across the Pacific, the line of the coast faintly visible, like a meandering smear brushed in with purple ink. We stayed there only long enough to see the rising sun dissipate the miracle, and then slid down over the grit again, reaching Tokyo in the evening. I wish, however, that I had not climbed Mount Fuji; never again was I able quite to capture the feeling of pristine beauty that it undoubtedly gives until such times as one actually sets foot upon its slopes. But then, as one of my Japanese friends was fond of saying, Fuji is only a " seeing ' mountain; it was never meant to be climbed. The Japanese, however, have a saying that there are two kinds of fool; those who have never climbed Mount Fuji, and those who have climbed it more than once.

In recent years the ascent of Fuji has become exceedingly popular with the members of patriotic societies. The mountain has always been regarded with a sort of religious awe, and the ascent to its summit counts almost as a pilgrimage. It is only natural, then, that the promoters of nationalistic sentiment should have seized the opportunity of infusing a political flavour into the already existing atmosphere of mysticism. Hardly a day now passes during the summer without some society or other passing a resolution on the summit. During the months before I left Japan the ascent was once made by a party of blind men; but perhaps the most astonishing of all was the pilgrimage carried out by soldiers totally incapacitated in the China war, most of whom had to be carried all the way. The purpose of this journey was to reaffirm their belief in Japan's holy war.

★ *16* ★

WITH THE EXCEPTION OF CRICKET, THE JAPANESE HAVE TAKEN TO every form of Western games and sport, but unlike us they do not make a tyranny of them, there being no compulsory games in Japanese schools. Baseball is the most popular game. It is practised everywhere; in streets, alleys, and waste plots, anywhere in fact where two or three boys happen to be gathered together. It was some time before I could be persuaded to take any interest in the game. Like most Englishmen I had always imagined it to be an inferior kind of cricket; and as for the latter game, it has always appeared to me to be the most boring method of killing time yet invented. I have loathed it ever since my school days, and nothing, not even a pre-war " cricket luncheon," would now induce me to attend a match. But a good game of baseball is a thrilling spectacle; and, once the rules have been mastered, quite the most exciting of all games to watch.

It was introduced into Japan in 1872 by two American teachers, since when the game has developed greatly. The professional teams, of which there are now quite a number, cannot be compared with their American counterparts, but Japanese and American University baseball teams are more or less on a par. The highlight of the season

GAMES AND SPORTS

is the so-called Six-University League, which is held twice every year in Tokyo, once in spring and again in the autumn. This takes place in the huge Meiji Stadium, which can accommodate some 50,000 spectators, and was built for the Olympic Games, which, but for the war, would have been held in Japan in 1940. I used regularly to attend these games between the six leading universities, obtaining from them the same sort of pleasure that one gets in watching the ballet; the joy of observing the human body completely under control. I remember on one occasion, early in May, 1940, being present at a particularly exciting game that had to be stopped on account of sudden rain. The German advance into Holland had been announced that morning, and I had felt an urgent need of something to take my mind off the horrors which I knew were being perpetrated. But I could not concentrate on the game, and when the stadium emptied I remained on alone, hypnotized by the sight of sodden and discarded newspapers flapping from the empty seats. And then I became fascinated by the pool of water which spread fanwise over the diamond, creeping silently towards the outfield, seeing in it a resemblance to the broken dykes of Europe. It seemed impossible, even at this distance, to escape from realities nearer home.

Of purely Japanese sports, the form of wrestling known as *Sumo* is the most popular. It is confined almost entirely to professionals, and in Japanese life occupies the same sort of position that boxing does with us. It attracts, too, a similar kind of audience, numbering among its patrons many women and members of the aristocracy.

The wrestlers are all huge men with gross protruding stomachs, and from an æsthetic point of view quite hideous. To the superficial observer they would appear to be suffering from severe prolapsis of the abdomen, but it seems that this abnormal enlargement of the belly is artificially produced, by means of gargantuan meals, the idea being that it gives a wrestler great advantages over a less well-developed opponent. I was only able to attend one tournament, when a Japanese friend took me with him to his box. As a rule it is difficult to gain admittance as the boxes are all in the possession of subscribers and to obtain an ordinary seat entails standing in an all-night queue, a proceeding I never thought worth while. I found the actual wrestling extremely boring. Each bout is decided in a very few seconds, but before the wrestlers come to grips they crouch, bowing and glaring at each other like a couple of outraged elephants. There was a time when these preliminaries could be almost indefinitely protracted, but it has now been laid down that the two opponents must come to grips within, I think, eight minutes. The result is decided as soon as one of the combatants has forced the other outside the ring. The

MARRIAGE

Japanese consider the preliminary stages enthralling, finding in them something akin to mysticism; but in order to appreciate the finer points of the sport it is necessary to be acquainted with it from early youth.

The *Sumo* hall is nevertheless a fascinating place, for it seems to exhale something of the spirit of old Japan. The outside of the building swarms with booths and portable eating houses, and nearly everyone wears Japanese dress. There is a constantly milling crowd of people, through which, every now and then, some famous wrestler " stomachs " his way, and the whole scene is lit by smoking flares. On entering one seems to step back several hundred years. The hall contains no seats, the whole of the huge audience being accommodated on the floor. The boxes, so-called, are small enclosures like sheep-pens, on the matting floor of which one squats. There were five other people in the one to which I was taken, and after half an hour I had lost all feeling in my lower limbs. It was not possible either to stand up or to ease the legs by stretching, since this would have disarranged the other occupants. The box had been lent to my host by a business acquaintance who wished to do him honour. We were consequently visited by a constant stream of attendants bearing boxes of food, tea and bottled beer, all of which had somehow to be stowed on the floor between us. The same procedure, more or less, seemed to be going on in all the other boxes. It was a bitterly cold day in early spring, and after consuming a couple of bottles of beer, which I certainly did not want, I felt an urgent need to leave the hall. This, however, I could not do without disturbing the whole party. Towards evening, as the tournament drew to a close, a large part of the audience seemed to be more or less intoxicated; the atmosphere was hilarious, and the spectators seemed to be paying less and less attention to the performance. When at last it came to an end I was not at first able to stand up, so severe was the cramp in my legs, but apart from the physical discomfort I had thoroughly enjoyed myself. The atmosphere was something like what I imagine that of the old-fashioned English music-hall to have been.

★ *17* ★

IN MY CONVERSATIONS WITH JAPANESE FRIENDS THE SUBJECT OF MARriage would, sooner or later, inevitably crop up. To marry is considered a duty, and no Japanese, not even the most emancipated, is able to recognize any excuse for not marrying. Nor did I ever quite succeed in convincing even my most intimate friends that I was a bachelor; they preferred to believe that I had reasons of my own for concealing my marriage. It was the one subject on which we were never able to agree.

Marriage among the Japanese is less of a personal and more of a family affair than it is in the West. It has been said that religion does not enter into the matter; but the chief motive for marriage, the overwhelming desire to preserve the continuity of the family, is in itself religious, being intimately bound up with ancestor worship. An Englishman does not as a rule allow his family to choose his wife for him; he makes his own choice. This is not so in Japan, nor is the contract difficult to terminate. The joint request and consent of the contracting parties is sufficient. The somewhat degrading proceedings which are a necessary preliminary to obtaining a divorce in England are unknown in Japan. The formal request for separation is usually made by the man; not because it is easier for the man to obtain divorce, but because, from the Japanese point of view, it would be unseemly in a woman to divorce her husband. She could not do so without arousing the unfavourable comment of her friends and relations.

As soon as their child, whether it be boy or girl, reaches a marriageable age, the parents select a suitable partner, or rather they entrust the matter to a go-between, choosing some discreet married man who is an intimate friend of the family. The preliminary conversations may last many months since, obviously, this is a matter which must be approached with the greatest delicacy. The go-between not only negotiates the marriage, but remains throughout life a sort of godfather to the young couple, and it is to him they refer in any case of dispute. If it is only a trivial matter he arbitrates; but sometimes he finds himself called upon to arrange a divorce. His is a somewhat thankless office, for if the marriage turns out unsatisfactorily he will probably be abused by both families.

To be a successful go-between calls for considerable tact and patience, for he will naturally not broach the actual subject of marriage until he has been able to find out the most intimate details, financial and otherwise, from his opposite number. When these preliminaries have been completed it is arranged that the prospective bride and bridegroom shall meet. Strict etiquette demands that this meeting take place at the go-between's own house; but except among the aristocracy it is nowadays usually held in public. During the time I was in Japan it had become rather fashionable among the middle classes to hold these " mutual seeing " parties in the Imperial Hotel and generally at tea time. I never ceased to be fascinated by the strange spectacle of some dozen or so Japanese seated stiffly round the table, all behaving with the strictest formality and bowing to each other on the slightest provocation. Besides the parents of the boy and girl concerned, a varied assortment of uncles and aunts, and the respective go-betweens, would be present. While the latter were doing their best to keep some sort of conversation going, the boy and girl, from opposite ends of the table, would eye each other furtively, but unless the two families happened to be exceptionally unconventional they would not be given an opportunity to talk to one another. In the fullness of time the party would terminate with more bowing and scraping, but the object of holding the meeting would not, of course, have been mentioned. On return to their respective homes the boy and girl are free to announce their decisions. In theory either is at liberty to object to the proposed marriage, and there the matter ends until a new candidate is produced. In actual practice, however, the young people are very much in their parents' hands and neither is likely to raise any objection ; certainly not the girl, for girls are not supposed to have any minds of their own.

If both parties approve, the marriage presents are exchanged. This corresponds to a betrothal, to which custom gives nearly all the binding force of a wedding. Among the lower classes indeed the exchange of presents is regarded as marriage ; and even should no further ceremony be performed the children born to a betrothed pair are not considered illegitimate.

The selection of the actual wedding day is a matter of some consideration since it must be fixed in accordance with the horoscopes of the respective parties. Only the more progressive Japanese venture to disregard this superstition. The wedding takes place at the home of the bridegroom's parents, where a dinner party is given, the distinguishing feature of which is what is known as the *san-san ku-do* or " three three, nine times " owing to the fact that both bride and bridegroom drink three times out of each of three wine-cups of different sizes. Only relatives and the go-betweens are present at the party, which in the case of members of the middle and upper classes is followed immediately by a banquet which is attended not only by those who were present at the drinking ceremony but by all the other friends and more distant relatives of the bride and bridegroom. The banquet is generally held at an hotel and is usually served in European style. European morning dress is worn by all the male guests, but it is usual for the women to wear Japanese costumes of strictly formal design. Wedding presents are sent to the bride before the wedding, and every guest, as he leaves the banquet, is presented with a souvenir of the occasion. These vary with the wealth of the bridegroom's parents and may be anything from a bouquet of flowers to some small specimen of Japanese art, a small lacquer box, for example. The banquet is nowadays often followed by a honeymoon, but this, I believe, is an innovation for which the West is responsible.

With none of this is the State concerned. A marriage in its legal aspect is determined in a very different manner. The head of the family to which the girl formerly belonged must go to the district office and notify the authorities that her registration should be transferred to the office of the district in which her husband lives. As soon as official intimation is received that the transfer has been carried out, the marriage is legally recognized.

When a parent has no son but only daughters it is usual for the bridegroom to be adopted into his wife's family, for no woman can be the legal head of a family. This illustrates again the importance which is attached to the preservation of the family line. In such cases the bridegroom drops his own family name and takes that of his wife. None but very poor men are willing to allow themselves to be adopted into their wife's family so that it is difficult for a family consisting only of daughters, unless it happens to be exceptionally rich, to attract good partners. Not infrequently, the difficulty is overcome by the adoption of male children. Large families are quite common, and a father is sometimes not unwilling to part with one of his sons, especially to a relative who is perhaps able to give the boy a better start in life than he can himself afford. But the custom of adoption often leads to awkward situations. For instance, one boy whom I knew had been adopted as a baby by his uncle, who was childless. Years later, the man's wife unexpectedly gave birth to a son, whereupon the boy's uncle, naturally wishing to make his own child his legal heir, attempted to return the adopted son to his real father, who was none too pleased at the way things were turning out.

Adoption sometimes leads to situations which look strange to us. It may happen that a man wishes to divorce his wife, but is anxious to show the world that he bears her no ill will. He divorces her and takes her as an adopted daughter. I know an interesting case where a man developed a great affection for the son of his dead brother and wished to make this child his heir. Unfortunately the boy was younger than his own son, so that he could not become the presumptive head of the family. In order to overcome the difficulty, the man first divorced his wife and then adopted her as his daughter, thus turning his own son into his grandson and making it possible for his nephew, whom he then adopted, to become his legal heir.

MARRIAGE

Asked if Japanese marriages turned out happily I should have no hesitation in saying that as many of them were successful as with us. There are, I think, two reasons for this. In the first place, the Japanese do not connect love with marriage in the way that we do. Very often, of course, love does develop; but the object of marriage is the procreation of children and, to a lesser extent, the preservation and strengthening of the family position. It is, moreover, not usual for young married men, unless they happen to be exceptionally rich, to set up homes of their own, and it is considered of great importance to select a wife who will " fit in " well with her husband's relations. The second reason is that Japanese women are exceptionally submissive. They are taught from early childhood that their main duty in life is to serve their husbands. When marriages go wrong as, of course, they sometimes do, it is nearly always due to the treatment a wife receives from her husband's mother. Many of these old women are positive viragos. After spending a life of drudgery in the service of their husbands they make it their main pleasure in life to oppress their daughters-in-law, whom they treat, if they can, as servants. But it is not true that the Japanese woman is little better than a slave. They are not, to be sure, given the same educational advantages as men; but it is at least doubtful if many of them wish to see their status changed. They feel very strongly that their place is in the home, but, the Japanese social system being what it is, there are very few spinsters, and women do not feel the same urge to compete with men as they do in European countries.

Most married men, if they can afford it, keep a mistress. No attempt is made at concealment. When a man has been married for a long time his wife and his mistress sometimes live together under his roof. This does not cause the friction it undoubtedly would with us, and quite often the two women become great friends. If the wife is a little jealous (although this is markedly uncharacteristic of Japanese married women), she obtains satisfaction from the fact that hers is the superior position, and that she, not the other woman, is the mother of her husband's heir. No Japanese man is expected to be faithful to his wife, but if my information is correct wives are very rarely unfaithful. There is a Japanese proverb which describes the essentials of a comfortable life as " A foreign style house, Chinese food, and a Japanese wife," and certainly it is the Japanese woman's outstanding faithfulness and obedience that has led so many observers to eulogize her.

GEISHA AND PROSTITUTION

⋆ *18* ⋆

NO ACCOUNT OF JAPANESE SOCIAL LIFE WOULD BE COMPLETE WITHOUT some reference to the Geisha, about whom a great deal of sentimental nonsense has been written. The Geisha is not, as is popularly supposed, a prostitute, although most of them have special admirers with whom they live; but they are not promiscuous. They must, of course, be pretty, and are taught from an early age to exploit their physical attractions; but their primary duty is to entertain the male, and no purely Japanese function is considered complete without them. They do not appear at any party at which ladies are present. It is customary for them to serve the guests with wine, chatter with them, and, at the end of the meal, entertain the company with singing and dancing. On the few occasions when I was forced to attend Geisha parties I found them extremely boring, for the feminine charm so lavishly displayed is of the kind that positively insults the intelligence. No offence is caused, however, if one fails to respond, and it can at least be said of Geisha that their presence saves one from having to make small-talk. Those who seek in female company nothing more than extreme elegance and an exaggerated feminity find them utterly captivating; their appeal is entirely to the senses, not to the mind. I have a suspicion that many Japanese themselves find them boring; but that cannot be admitted, for they are a part of the national tradition.

The training of a Geisha begins when she is about seven years of age, but for a very long time she is little more than an attendant on her elders. It has been said that many parents sell their daughters to the owners of Geisha houses in return for a lump sum, but this is not quite true. What the parents do is to sign a long-term contract, in return for which they receive an advance on their daughter's eventual earnings. The owners of Geisha houses are not philanthropists, and as the training of a Geisha takes a good many years and calls for a considerable expenditure on clothes, they can hardly be blamed for ensuring a good return on their money. The girls receive on an average fifteen per cent of their earnings, and not many of them are able to save enough to pay back the original advance made to their parents. Until this is done they remain legally bound and cannot give up the profession. A Geisha, however, is generally able to find a rich admirer who is willing to buy her out. She cannot, of course, marry until she is free from her legal obligations, or until such time as advancing years make it no longer profitable to retain her services. It sometimes happens that a Geisha makes a marriage with a man of good family; but the majority of them eventually become the owners of restaurants, bars or tea-shops, for a man who has taken a Geisha as his mistress will usually set her up in business when she no longer has any further attraction for him. Some of the most exclusive restaurants in Tokyo are owned and managed by women who in their day have been famous Geisha.

Geisha are, however, an expensive hobby and the whole business is one of the greatest rackets in Japan. They cannot be employed at the actual " Geisha House " where they live, so that it is necessary to engage a room in what is known as a *Machiai*, or " Waiting House," so called because it is here that the Geisha wait for their employer, or vice versa. The use of a room in a *Machiai* costs anything from eight to twenty-four shillings for a period of a few hours, to which must be added the cost of any food and drinks consumed. The Geisha themselves are paid from six to thirty shillings for each period of two hours or less. The most famous ones are able to demand higher fees, and are paid as much as three pounds for a theoretical two hours. Those at the top of the profession are in such demand that in actual practice they seldom spend more than fifteen minutes or so at any one party (unless their employer at the moment happens himself to be a man of considerable fame and position). In addition to these disbursements there is now a government luxury-tax as well, which is levied both on the rent of the room and on the fees payable to the girls. Just before I left the country this tax had risen by degrees to 100 per cent; and according to a recent German broadcast from Tokyo (reported in the *Evening Standard* on the 18th January, 1943), " new stringent measures " have since been introduced. " They include heavy increases in taxes, including that on cigarettes, which has already been increased four times, and a new and heavy tax on Geisha houses."

Every town in Japan has its proportion of Geisha. Statistics are not available, but in Tokyo alone there are certainly many thousands of them. The girls live in houses in specially allotted quarters of the city, and the whole business is controlled by a huge central organization, which is in effect a sort of monopoly.

The Geisha racket is an exploitation of snobbery. A great many Japanese, and particularly those of the younger generation, do not take any particular pleasure in them, but a man's position is to some extent assessed by the number and quality of Geisha he provides for the entertainment of his guests.

GEISHA AND PROSTITUTION

Of great sociological interest is the effect the Geisha system has had on Westernized forms of entertainment in Japan. There are in Tokyo, for instance, literally thousands of so-called tea rooms. These are for the most part patronized by students and young business men. Most of them are exactly what their names imply; places where one can spend an hour or so drinking tea, listening to the inevitable gramophone, or reading the papers. A certain number of these places, however, are classed as "Special tea-rooms," because they also provide girls for the entertainment of the guests. Unlike Geisha, these girls do not receive any training, and their entertainment consists solely in sitting and talking with the guests. I went by chance to one of the most notorious of these places on my second night in Tokyo, and I shall always remember it since it provided one of the most embarrassing experiences of my life. Noticing what I thought was a restaurant, lit up like a gin palace and echoing with sounds of laughter, I decided to enter. I was immediately led to a table in a shaded alcove, and before there was time to decide what to order a young lady appeared and perched herself on my knee. I did not, of course, at that time know a word of Japanese; and as for the English of the girl who had attached herself to me, it consisted of but two phrases, "I rab yiu" (I love you), and "Thenk yiu; plise kom agen," which she kept on repeating, accompanying the phrase with nervous giggles. Obtaining no response to this earnest protestation, after about a quarter of an hour she slipped off my knee, went away and returned with the bill. I paid it thankfully and made my escape. Since the war these "Special tea-rooms" have been forbidden to students as an austerity measure, but there is nothing to prevent a student from entering, provided he is not wearing his school uniform, and they remain one of the most popular forms of cheap entertainment in Japan. They are, I imagine, a modern development of the traditional Geisha entertainment.

The Yoshiwara, which takes pride of place in the sight-seeing tourist's programme is, as every schoolboy knows, Tokyo's most famous brothel quarter, and houses many thousands of prostitutes. It is elaborately organized and very strictly controlled. Until comparatively recently the girls used to sit about on the ground floor or in front of the houses to exhibit their charms, but this has now been stopped. Photographs are displayed instead, just as they are put up outside theatres and cinemas in this country. One strolls round looking at the portraits, makes a choice and then goes to the office to inquire if the lady is free. If she is, one buys a ticket for the amount of time one wishes to spend with her. It is as easy as buying a ticket for a cinema. There is nothing furtive about it, nor is there anything sordid about the surroundings. Indeed most of the brothels are arranged with exquisite taste.

The Japanese are realists; they understand perfectly well that the prostitute occupies a definite place in capitalist society as it at present exists, and they have organized the profession on a hygienic and business basis. They run it as efficiently as they run any other commercial concern. Although narrow-minded in some respects, the Japanese do at least recognize the sexual needs of the man, and Japan is probably the only country in the world where a respectable woman runs no risk of being accosted on the streets at night. And the streets, of course, are free from wandering prostitutes.

★ *19* ★

THE TRADITIONAL THEATRE IS OF GREAT IMPORTANCE TO THE STUDENT of Japanese manners, for on the stage alone is it still possible to observe the old life of the country. The Japanese drama would appear to have developed out of religious dances, which were accompanied by some sort of chorus from very early times. At the beginning of the fifteenth century some of the more cultivated Buddhist priests, with the encouragement of the aristocracy, began to take an active interest in these performances. Special edifices, half temple half open-air theatres, were erected in the courtyards of many of the bigger shrines, and thus the peculiar type of performance known as *Noh*, a word which is generally translated as " Accomplishment," came into being. The chorus, characteristic of the older type of performance, was retained, but an addition was made in the shape of two personages who recited some of the more dramatic portions of the verse in order to enhance their effect. The history of the *Noh* parallels in many ways the development of the drama in England; our own morality plays, for instance, came into being in much the same way. There is, however, one great difference: whereas the English morality play was intended for the masses, the *Noh* was a strictly aristocratic performance. It made no appeal to the uneducated, who could not indeed even understand its language, and for this reason it survives to this day in approximately its original form.

I think I am correct in saying that there are no professional *Noh* actors in the strict sense of the term, by which I mean that most of the players are supported by wealthy patrons. The performances are given by families who have handed down the art from father to son for more than four hundred years. These groups of family players interpret the plays in different ways, and thus we find the existence of six main " schools "; but this is a matter for the expert, and I do not propose to touch on it here.

Noh plays are performed in special theatres, of which there are in Tokyo alone about a couple of dozen. The play is performed on a highly-polished wooden stage of regulation size, built above the ground, eighteen feet square. The stage is open on three sides and has a narrow extension on one side for the singers, and another at the back for the musicians. To the rear extension a passage, known as the " Flower Bridge," is attached. It is along this bridge that the players make their entry on to the stage. There is neither drop-curtain nor scenery, but a representation of a pine tree is painted on the wooden panelling at the rear of the stage.

The auditorium is arranged something like the interior of a Japanese house. There are no seats, but the floor is covered by the usual soft matting, on which the spectators squat. Most of the audience, for their own comfort, usually wear Japanese dress. The *Noh* to-day, even more than in the past, is a somewhat esoteric entertainment, making no appeal to the ordinary playgoer. It is attended by people who come primarily not to be amused, but to be instructed. Most of them follow the performance text in hand, for the language, although exceedingly beautiful, is archaic and difficult to comprehend, especially when chanted. It differs from modern Japanese to about the same extent that, say, *Piers Plowman* differs from the English of the present day.

I always found it a great strain to attend a *Noh* performance. Apart from the discomfort of squatting on the floor, it is difficult to concentrate when one does not understand a word of what is being said. To have read the text is little help, for in most of the plays there is little plot or action, the whole charm lying in the beauty of the language. So that unless one is an amateur of the *Noh* the performance does undoubtedly cause a feeling of boredom. The actors, once they have arrived at the centre of the stage, seldom move from one position, and the action of the play, such as it is, advances very slowly. Mr. Bernard Shaw, when he visited the country some years ago, was naturally taken to see a *Noh* play, for this is considered the highest form of Japanese artistic achievement. And he has never been forgiven for having fallen asleep during the performance. I never went quite as far as this, but there were times when I found it difficult to keep awake.

The music makes no appeal to my musical sense, although I must concede that it possesses a certain weird charm, and produces at times a feeling of suspense and even horror. It is completely different from ordinary Japanese music. It affects me as more "Oriental" than any other Eastern music I have ever heard.

The dresses used are gorgeous. Many of them have been handed down from one generation to another and are of great historical value. They are highly prized by their owners, who will never in any circumstances part with them.

With a few exceptions the actors in a *Noh* play appear in masks. These masks are somewhat smaller than the natural size of the human face and have very small eye-holes, which are difficult to see through. It is this fact, I imagine, that causes the plays to move so slowly, for the masked actor has only a very limited field of vision. He advances on to the stage slowly and deliberately, walking almost like a blind man, and as much as fifteen minutes may elapse between his first appearance on the "Bridge" and his reaching the centre of the stage.

Some scholars have seen in the Japanese *Noh* masks certain affinities with the masks used in ancient Greek drama, but in actual fact there are many points of difference, some of them fundamental. The Greek mask was invented to enable actors quickly to change their parts. This was necessary, as in early Greek drama the number of players was limited to three. Then, too, the theatres were very big. Some of them are known to have accommodated as many as three thousand spectators. In order to be effective the masks had to be large and their expressions exaggerated, for otherwise the effects they were intended to produce would not have been visible to the more distant spectators.

Japanese *Noh* masks, on the other hand, have been developed without reference to theatrical requirements. The plays, with rare exceptions, have always been performed in small, intimate theatres, holding at most a few hundreds. Even to-day in Tokyo the largest *Noh* theatre does not seat more than seven hundred, the others having accommodation for only half that number or even less. It is for this reason that there was never any need for undue exaggeration in the expression given to the masks. The artists who carved them were well aware that their products would be observed at close quarters, and they tried to make them equal to such a severe test. The carving of *Noh* masks is an hereditary craft, and the best specimens are much sought after by collectors of Japanese art. Quite apart from their use as an integral part of stage costume, they are regarded as objects of art in themselves.

The *Noh* mask has one feature which is unique. Although the Japanese proverbially liken expressionless human features to a *Noh* mask, the latter yet has an exceptional capacity for suggesting changes of expression; one and the same mask may be used to express both melancholy and cheerfulness.

If a mask is taken in the hand or laid on a table and carefully examined it will be found devoid of all expression. But when it is worn by a skilled actor and inclined in a certain way this has the effect of imparting a living expression: and it is really extraordinary how the same mask can be used, by merely changing the angle at which the light falls on it, to produce widely different effects. These varying effects are largely possible as a result of the peculiar carving of the lips, which are shaped like a flower in bud. When the mask is viewed directly from the front the lips appear half opened; but when it is turned slightly downwards they appear fully closed. If the mask is slightly tilted upwards the lips will appear to be softened by a smile; in fact almost any effect can be produced.

As *Noh* plays are performed without the use of scenery it is necessary to give the audience some idea of the scene in which the action is supposed to be taking place. There are many conventions for suggesting a scene, in some of which the mask plays a part. For instance, where fallen flower petals are supposed to be floating on the surface of a running stream, the actor tilts his mask slightly upwards and shakes his head. Similarly, the flashing of the mask from side to side denotes fireflies flitting about in the darkness of a summer evening. To the casual visitor these conventions, of which there are a great many, mean nothing; but to the initiate they present no difficulties, and are as meaningful as actual language.

A typical *Noh* performance occupies the greater part of a day and consists of a number of different plays, each lasting about an hour. Some of the most famous of the plays are exceedingly gloomy, and it is usual to intersperse comediettas and classical dances between them. At one time these comic interludes, the humour of which is often broad, were performed in colloquial language, and this is the origin of the popular form of traditional Japanese drama. But the language of the *Kabuki*, as it is called, although understood by the majority of the audience, is not the ordinary speech of the present day. It differs from modern Japanese about as much as the more obscure parts of Shakespeare differ from our language in this century.

The *Kabuki* came into existence early in the seventeenth century, at about the same time as the *ukiyoye*, or genre wood-block print. In fact *ukiyoye* artists have always sought inspiration in the theatre, some of the best known prints being portraits of *Kabuki* actors.

The appeal of the *Kabuki* is primarily to the masses, and the plays fall into two well-marked groups. There are historical dramas, in which much emphasis is laid upon loyalty, and comic pieces, usually of a somewhat erotic nature. The scene of the latter is more often than not laid in the Yoshiwara, Tokyo's famous brothel quarter.

A typical *Kabuki* programme contains three or four plays of different types; it begins at four o'clock in the afternoon, and usually lasts for about six hours. The majority of the audience dines in one or other of the numerous restaurants which are situated in the actual theatre building. The principal *Kabuki* theatre in Tokyo is built in Western style and is about the same size as one of the bigger London playhouses. Until comparatively recently the theatres were not furnished with seats, and the audience squatted on the matted floor as it still does at *Sumo* tournaments. In those days the general atmosphere, a sense of which is vividly conveyed by some of Hiroshige's colour prints, cannot have been very different from that which fills the *Sumo* hall. Although the present theatre is modern its numerous corridors are crowded with old-fashioned booths of every description, but a modern note is provided by several restaurants and even a photographer's studio. In the old days these stalls would have been outside the theatre, but during the intervals between the plays the milling crowd helps one to visualize what the place was like before it was modernized.

The profession of *Kabuki* actor is in most cases hereditary. Sons of actors succeed their fathers in the profession, and those without sons usually adopt the child of some other actor, giving him their own stage name. There are no actresses in the *Kabuki*, and the actors who specialize in the impersonation of women devote years of study to feminity; indeed they are more consistently feminine than women. As a result of this the *Kabuki* theatre is much patronized by Geisha, who attend the performances not so much for amusement as to learn correct feminine deportment. Some of the best known actors play only female parts, but a really great artist such as the present Kikugoro (the sixth to inherit the name) is as skilful in male parts as in female.

The *Kabuki* is primarily a visual entertainment, although dialogue is chanted and an orchestra with vocalists, seated to one side of the stage, plays very much the same role as that of the chorus in classical Greek drama, by aiding the action with explanations. The life and thought, costumes and manners, of all classes of feudal society are well illustrated on the *Kabuki* stage. The scenery used at the present day is extremely realistic and nothing is left to the imagination; the production may well be compared with that for which the old Lyceum was once famous. But together with this extremely realistic background there are a number of stage conventions which strike the Western visitor as extremely incongruous. For instance, the actors frequently change their costumes while on the stage. In this they are assisted by their dressers, who wear black clothing, a sign that they are taking no part in the play and should be disregarded by the audience. Similarly, properties are brought on to the stage while a scene is actually in progress, and taken away again when they are no longer required. The special attendants who do this work are also dressed in black and known as *kurombo*, a word meaning negro.

As in the *Noh* theatre the *Kabuki* also has a " Flower Bridge," but in the latter it consists of a long narrow platform at one side which stretches right through the audience from the stage to the rear of the auditorium. The " Bridge " is generally chosen by the actors for their best entrances and exits, but it is used most effectively in the case of processions. It is not unlikely that the modern " gangplank," at one time popular in Western revue theatres, was copied from Japan ; and certainly the revolving stage was a feature of the *Kabuki* long before it was used in any other country, for I have myself seen old prints in which the scene is shown being turned round by a crowd of men pushing a sort of winch-like apparatus underneath the stage.

One does not need to understand a word of Japanese in order to appreciate the *Kabuki*. I have often heard complaints that it is dull and boring, but I have noticed that the foreigner who visits the theatre never leaves before the end of the performance. It is really a cross between a pageant and a ballet, and I doubt if the art of decor has been developed to such an extent anywhere else in the world. One of the elements in traditional Japanese acting that makes for monotony is the convention that no use must be made of facial expression. This convention, I believe, was taken over by the *Kabuki* from its precursor, the so-called doll theatre, in which all the parts were played by nearly life-sized puppets held by manipulators who, dressed in black, were actually on the stage. There is now only one doll theatre existing in Japan, the famous Bunraku-za in Osaka. The plays performed there are identical with those seen in the *Kabuki*, but the real connoisseur of Japanese drama prefers the former. The absence of dialogue and the comparatively stilted movements of the marionettes make for a formalism which is highly regarded. Moreover, the accompanying recitative is thought to be the best music of its kind in Japan. The Bunraku-za stands in a class by itself. The world-famous Italian marionette theatre cannot compare with it. It has influenced the *Kabuki* in many other ways, but these are matters for the specialist.

Some twenty years or so ago a " little theatre " movement was started in Tokyo, having as its object the production of Western plays in Japanese translation. The original company had a theatre of its own, at Tsukiji, a down-town quarter of Tokyo, but since then numerous other groups have come into existence. When I left Japan several of these companies were still in existence, but the spirit of the times was gradually forcing them off the stage, and they were being disbanded one by one. There was no actual ban on the production of foreign plays as such; but in Japan dramatic censorship is in the hands of the police, who have their own peculiar views on morality, and on what constitutes " dangerous thought." As a result of this the production of almost any modern play of ideas has now become impossible; even if sanction is granted for a production, the play has to be so much cut that what remains is barely intelligible. Ibsen fell under the ban, a license to produce *The Doll's House* being refused on the grounds that in these days of what the Japanese are pleased to call " spiritual mobilization " it gave women a wrong idea of their wifely duties.

In these modern plays the female parts are played by women. The production is the same as in Europe or America, but one very curious convention has arisen. It seems that in long-past times the foreigner, in the popular mind, was a person with red hair, as a result of which it has become customary for every member of the cast of a foreign play to be rigged out in a ginger wig. Until one gets used to it, this convention adds a somewhat sinister note. I well remember the first time I saw a Japanese performance of *Hamlet*, when I was obsessed by a dream-like feeling that all the characters were in some way incestuously related to one another.

Another theatrical innovation is the revue. This is the Japanese idea of a Broadway " leg-show "; but in view of what I have already said concerning the Japanese female leg, it would perhaps be kinder if I made no further comment. The only interesting feature of the Japanese revue is that it was started in opposition to the *Kabuki*; and since the *Kabuki* does not permit women to appear on its stage the revue contains no men, all the male parts being played by girls. Strangely enough, the revue does not seem to attract men in the least. The greater part of the audience consists of girls, and most of these in their early twenties. It is said that the actresses who specialize in male impersonation receive numerous letters from their admirers, and certainly I have myself often seen crowds of young girls waiting outside the stage door in order to catch a glimpse of their own particular favourite. This is strange, for in Japan members of the theatrical profession do not receive adulation as in other countries. For this there may be some Freudian explanation; it is possibly a psychological compensation for the absence of physical affection which is such a feature of Japanese social life, and particularly in the case of girls.

But the most popular form of entertainment in Japan at the present day is undoubtedly the cinema, in which, until the outbreak of war, American films held the leading place. In the days of the silent film a man used to stand at the side of the stage and explain to the audience what was happening, and this still goes on in some of the remote country districts. With the invention of the talkie this became unnecessary, a Japanese version of the English dialogue being superimposed on the screen.

Foreign films have always been very carefully censored, and the Japanese version is often far from faithful to the original. I remember seeing that admirable film *You Can't Take It With You*, in which much of the dialogue, being of a very socialistic nature, was not acceptable to the Japanese authorities. The action, however, was considered innocuous, so the difficulty was overcome by the simple expedient of leaving the offending passages untranslated.

The Japanese public is not allowed to see what I believe are technically known in Hollywood as " emotional close-ups "; the act of kissing is either omitted or so drastically telescoped that labial contact is not visible on the screen for more than a couple of seconds. To the Western reader this may seem absurdly prudish. To the Japanese, however, this is a question not so much of morality as of good taste. They regard any public manifestation of the sexual instinct as a breach of manners, believing, and rightly in my opinion, that even in the most harmless form, intimacies of this nature should be reserved for the privacy of the bedroom. During the whole of the four years I spent in the country I never once saw a man and woman even do so much as to walk arm in arm, and although I have now been back in England for some months I am still unable to accustom myself to the licence permitted in war-time London. The restraint of the Japanese is, in part at least, based upon a different view of the status of women. In this particular matter the Japanese mode of behaviour is, to my mind, very much more civilized than ours. There is, of course, nothing particularly Japanese about it; the same decorous manners rule in China or any other Oriental country.

In addition to the numerous American, and less numerous English films shown in Tokyo, a few other foreign films were shown. Two or three cinemas specialized in films from France and Germany, but the exhibition of Russian films is not permitted in Japan. The Italians have never gone in much for film production, and the only picture from Italy I ever saw in Tokyo was a documentary one about the Mediterranean entitled *Mare Nostrum*, which, somewhat infelicitiously, was being shown just at the time when news of the British raid on Taranto was made public. It caused even the Japanese audience to titter.

The Japanese have always been appreciative of the excellence of French films, in spite of the fact that few are able to understand the dialogue, but modern German films have never met with any popularity. This is in some part due to language difficulties, but more to a true perception of the fact that German films have deteriorated since the exodus of talent caused by the Nazi persecutions. Moreover, the great majority of modern German pictures are purely propagandist, and as such make no appeal to the Japanese. They get as much propaganda as they can stand in their own present-day productions.

The German film *Olympia*, a documentary dealing with the Olympic games held at Berlin in 1936, was, however, extremely successful. This film, of which there are a number of versions, has had a wide showing in different parts of the world. It has been very cleverly edited so as to bring the inhabitants of the particular country in which it is being shown into prominence. Thus the edition shown in Tokyo gave great prominence to the Japanese athletes and contained a number of shots picturing them being received by Mr. Hitler. But a German friend who had previously seen the film in Berlin told me that on that occasion the Japanese did not appear on the screen at all. *Sieg im Westen*, however, the film depicting the campaign in France, was by no means so successful, principally because great emphasis was laid on German plans for world conquest. This, quite naturally, did not meet with popular approval, and the film was withdrawn after a short run.

Outside the big towns the indigenous Japanese film is preferred to the foreign. A great many of these are film versions of traditional *Kabuki* plays, but in recent years there has been a tendency to produce more pictures with a modern setting. As one would expect, up-to-date Japanese films are remarkable chiefly for the use made of natural scenery and for the excellence of the photography. But the Japanese have not yet learnt how to use the mobile camera, nor do they understand the technique of cutting a film. Most Japanese pictures are consequently too long, a defect which, to the European mind, is characteristic of all Japanese entertainments. Deprived of stimulus

RADIO BROADCASTING

from outside by the exclusion of American and English films, Japanese pictures are likely to deteriorate. As with every other Japanese activity the film industry is now controlled by government; in the course of the last few months before I left the country the pure amusement film had practically disappeared, its place being taken by pictures in which the propaganda element swamped everything else.

★ *20* ★

RADIO BROADCASTING IN JAPAN IS UNDER THE CONTROL OF A SINGLE organization, the Broadcasting Corporation of Japan. This huge corporation is by way of being supervised by the Ministry of Communications, but actually all broadcasting is now controlled by the Information Bureau, which also performs the functions of a propaganda ministry. All programmes are subject to strict censorship and nothing that might harm the interests of the country and its people is allowed to go on the air. Even before the outbreak of war it was impossible to broadcast the proceedings of the Diet or any political speeches without authorization.

The first radio programme in Japan was broadcast in 1925, since when the service has been enormously extended. In 1936, the latest date for which reliable information is available, the number of licence holders was stated to have reached 2,776,189, which figure represents roughly forty per thousand of the population. At the present day the percentage must be very much higher for there is now hardly a household that does not own a set. The programmes start at six o'clock in the morning and continue until eleven at night, and during the whole of these seventeen hours nearly all the radio sets in the country are kept going at full blast. Radio is, in fact, one of the major curses of living in Japan. There is no escape from the noise; it assaults one from all directions. Moreover, the ordinary Japanese-made receiving set is extremely cheap (it costs on the average about the equivalent of thirty shillings), which means that the valves are of very poor quality, causing much distortion.

Nor is this all. Little attention has hitherto been paid to microphone technique, with the result that nearly every talk opens with a burst of thunder, the speaker clearing his throat. This is followed by frequent coughing and the crackle of pages being turned over. The daily programme, at the time of my departure, included at least three or four patriotic speeches by army officers, the majority of whom, to judge from the volume and quality of the sound, seemed to be addressing the microphone as though it were a body of troops being rallied to one last effort. I must say, however, that nobody seemed to pay much attention to these speeches; there is a limit to what even the Japanese will stand.

The first item in the daily programme consists of radio physical exercises, and this feature is repeated every few hours until the stations shut down at night. Finding that the desired reaction was not produced, the government started a campaign to popularize these exercises. Orders were issued that commercial firms should encourage their employees to participate by giving them the opportunity to do so during office hours, and I remember an occasion when going into a large office at about two o'clock one afternoon I found every member of the staff, from the manager downward, squatting in front of his desk in the "knees bend" position. I thought I must be interrupting some religious ceremony, until a further command from the loud speaker ordered the assembly on to its feet again.

A good deal of time is also devoted to the teaching of foreign languages over the air, and until the war there was a daily lesson in English, usually at six-thirty in the morning. I do not know if this is being continued, but certainly more radio time is now being devoted to German. News bulletins are read four times daily, and there are occasional relays of short-wave broadcasts from Germany and Italy. Most of these are excerpts from concerts or operatic performances, but Mr. Hitler's orations have been relayed on a number of occasions. Japanese music, story-telling and cultural talks made up most of the rest of the programmes, Western music being given only the "fill-up" times. There were often excellent programmes of gramophone records, but the "live" music was generally pure torture. For in order to provide variety nearly everyone in Japan who is able to extract some sort of noise from an instrument is sooner or later called to the microphone. I frequently had to listen to piano recitals given by a soloist who was still in the stage of fumbling for the notes. To switch off was quite useless; the first-year student's interpretation of Chopin (his almost inevitable choice) still tinkled its way through the lath and plaster walls of my house from all four quarters of the compass.

The Japanese do not manufacture a commercial short-wave receiver; nor do they allow any member of the general public to possess one. During my time a very powerful set was installed in the Foreign Office, and daily bulletins, containing extracts from all important British and American broadcasts were circulated confidentially to some of the higher officials. I was not, of course, allowed to see these bulletins, but I used occasionally to listen to a short-wave broadcast in one of the rooms where a set was available. There is also an official monitoring service, and certain of the more senior government servants are permitted to have their own short-wave sets. I should say that they number, at a conservative estimate, about five hundred.

It is important to realize how completely Japan is now cut off from the rest of the world. The people in general have no means of listening to foreign broadcasts. Clandestine listening, such as is known to be carried on in occupied Europe, is quite impossible in Japan. Before the war a few Japanese, mostly students, did indeed construct their own short-wave sets and listen secretly, but the penalties for this are now so great that no one dare take the risk; the Japanese are well aware of the consequences of falling into the hands of their own police.

In Europe, in order to listen to foreign broadcasts, a short-wave set is in most cases unnecessary. News from foreign stations can be picked up easily on the ordinary medium-wave set with which people are accustomed to listen to their home stations. This is not possible in Japan. The cheap Japanese sets are capable of no more than picking up the programmes radiated from the home stations. Nor is there any outside station near enough to reach Japan with a medium-wave transmission. It can thus be seen how easily the Japanese, probably more than any other nation in the world, can be kept from hearing outside news that their government wishes to conceal from them.

When I first arrived in Japan in 1938 the broadcasting studios were situated in a converted mansion, and there were none of the facilities one finds in a modern studio. Not one of the rooms was soundproof and loose wires trailed all over the floor. I talked once or twice to America from this building, usually at five-thirty in the morning, and before I got to the end I nearly always heard the gentleman in the next room clearing his throat and warming up prior to starting off the first programme of physical exercises. But in 1940 the Japan Broadcasting Corporation moved into its new headquarters, a modern building designed on the lines of our own Broadcasting House, and fitted up with all the latest apparatus. It was from this date that the Japanese started broadcasting to foreign countries on a big scale. But I have already made it clear that so far as Western entertainment is concerned there is a great dearth of talent in Japan; the only thing the Japanese can give the rest of the world is their own version of the news, for no one is likely to listen to a short-wave broadcast of a fifth-rate quartet taking liberties with Schubert when he can hear a first-class orchestra playing from his own home station.

I used sometimes to produce Japanese plays in English translation for the American transmission, but I cannot believe that many people listened to them. No professional actors were available and I had generally to fall back on such of my friends and acquaintances as happened to have nothing else to do on that particular day; sometimes I played one or two of the parts myself. The Japanese are not yet very advanced in the technique of dramatic production; and whereas in London most of the sound effects are now produced by means of records, we had to work in a studio cluttered up with attendants and bits of machinery to make the necessary noises. I remember on one occasion producing a play the action of which was supposed to take place at nightfall beside a running stream. There were six characters in the play, and we were hardly able to move because, in order to produce a realistic atmosphere, the Japanese assistant producer insisted on having in the studio several men to make a churning noise with tubs of water and a number of live cicadas in small wicker cages to chirp throughout the action. This performance was particularly memorable because in the middle of it there was an agonized cry of " Oh God ! The grasshoppers have got loose ! " from one of the female performers ; and I had some difficulty in making the cicada-keeper realize that the play could go on all the same.

★ *21* ★

THE YOUNGER GENERATION IN JAPAN IS INTENSELY INTERESTED IN Western music; in fact many people have been accustomed to listen to it from their earliest years. To such, their own Japanese music sounds as foreign as it does to Europeans. This interest in Western music has spread widely of late, the war being to a great extent responsible. The danger that attaches to too keen an interest in foreign literature and philosophy is not incurred by the lover of Occidental music. The Japanese police have yet to prove that there is anything corrupting in listening even to the *morceaux* of, say, Mr. Albert Ketelby.

A great many concerts of one sort or another are held in present-day Japan, many of them fifth-rate or worse. The audiences, except for a sprinkling of critics and professional musicians, consist almost entirely of young people, and I always felt that they afforded one of the most pathetic sights in the country. They will listen to an inferior performance of some seldom-heard work with rapt attention, realizing that it is bad, but knowing that they cannot in present circumstances hope to hear anything better. Before the war most of the international celebrities visited Japan in the course of their tours, but for the last six or seven years the country has been cut off from the rest of the world, musically as well as in every other way.

The musical life of Japan centres round the concerts given regularly by the New Symphony Orchestra, which was formed originally by Viscount Hidemaro Konoye, the younger brother of a former Prime Minister. A few years after its inception, however, Viscount Konoye resigned and went to Germany, where he still occasionally conducts a performance given by the Berlin Philharmonic Orchestra. He is probably the best musician Japan has so far produced and has made some exceedingly interesting transcriptions of the *Gagaku*, the ancient Japanese court music, at least one of which, *Etanraku*, has been played by orchestras in all parts of the world. Incidentally, *Gagaku*, which originated in China, is harmonic, and this makes it the only type of Japanese music capable of development. It has much in common with modern atonal music.

After the departure of Viscount Konoye, the New Symphony Orchestra had a number of foreign conductors, but it never made much progress. Even in normal times of peace the Japanese finds little inducement to cultivate any musical gifts he may possess, and the country has produced no first-class conductor. But with the advent of the Nazi regime in Germany large numbers of good musicians were glad of any opportunity to escape. The Tokyo orchestra was lucky in securing the services of Herr Josef Rosenstock, at one time a pupil of Toscanini and a musician who would not in ordinary circumstances have found it necessary to leave Europe in order to find employment. During the period of his conductorship the New Symphony Orchestra has improved out of all recognition. It is not yet capable of giving a first-class performance, but it is doing a great service in making the classics, together with the best work of contemporary composers, known to the Japanese public. By 1940 Rosenstock's concerts had become so popular that in order to meet the public demand every one of them had to be repeated on two consecutive nights; even so, many people had to be turned away.

The German community in Tokyo could not, of course, attend these concerts since Mr. Rosenstock was not of pure Aryan descent, but there was a rival orchestra, whose blonde conductor had come out to Japan at the instigation of the Reich. But all the efforts of the German Embassy could do nothing to popularize his concerts, which indeed were markedly inferior, and at no performance was more than a quarter of the hall filled. The Japanese musical public is still limited in numbers, but what there is of it is critical.

The year 1940 was celebrated throughout Japan as the 2,600th anniversary of the accession to the throne of the first Emperor, Jimmu Tenno, who is alleged to have commenced his reign in 660 B.C. However this may be, the government commissioned several well-known foreign musicians to write special compositions in honour of the occasion. Some declined the honour, but scores were received from England, Germany, France, and Italy. As an official of the Foreign Office I received an invitation to the concert at which these compositions were performed for the first time in public. It was held in the huge *Kabuki* theatre, and in order to do justice to the occasion the New Symphony Orchestra was augmented by the inclusion of practically every living Japanese musician; it must have been well over two hundred strong, but as this was a diplomatic occasion Mr. Rosenstock was debarred from conducting. The concert opened with the playing of the Japanese National Anthem in full, throughout which the Axis representatives remained in the "Heil Hitler" position, much to the discomfort of those seated immediately in front of them. The French had submitted a suite by Jacques Ibert, but the chief item of the concert was the "Festival Music" of Richard Strauss. This is scored for a gigantic orchestra and contains parts for special drums, temple bells, gongs and various other exotic instruments. I was looking forward to hearing this, but it turned out to be a sterile composition. Although technically clever, it gave me the impression of being a piece of patchwork containing rejected passages from most of Strauss's earlier works.

To my disappointment the concert was a purely Axis occasion. This was not intended. It was due to an unfortunate occurrence which it was not possible to make public. Mr. Benjamin Britten had agreed to submit a composition, but the letter inviting him to do so was apparently badly worded in that he was asked to write something *in memory* of the defunct Emperor, and no hint was given that the occasion was a joyful one. Not unnaturally, Mr. Britten submitted a dirge. Unknown, I imagine, to him, experiments were made in altering the tempo, but no matter what liberties were taken with the score, there was still very obviously nothing festive about it. It was decided that his composition could not be performed; but in order to save the face of all those concerned it was made known that the English offering had not been received in time to permit of adequate rehearsal. In actual fact, it was the first to be submitted. Mr. Britten's extremely moving composition, now named *Sinfonia da Requiem*, has since been performed in this country, where it has received the praise that it merits, but I believe it would have been even more appreciated in Japan since its atonal writing has much in common with the Japanese *Gagaku*, to which I have already referred.

The Japanese have produced a number of pianists, most of them women, but none even of the second rank. Most of them were trained in Europe, but left before reaching the virtuoso stage. In their own country they now enjoy a reputation which is out of all proportion to their accomplishments, for by European standards they are in truth little better than gifted amateurs. But as with every other subject, so with music: the Japanese are inclined to believe that once they have mastered the technique there is nothing more to be learned. What they lack is the ability to interpret music, and this, I think, they are not likely to acquire until Western music has become an integral part of their culture. There is now an intense interest in the subject, but I cannot help feeling that even the most sensitive Japanese is at present incapable of receiving the emotional stimulus that a European gets from hearing some great work. Indeed, seeing how different our music is from theirs, it is surprising that the Japanese should have taken to it at all.

Of Japanese composers it is unnecessary to say more than that they have not so far written anything of value. Most of their compositions are inspired by trivial European models and are of the "Temple Bells" variety. I have not made a deep study of Japanese music, but it seems to me that in Japan the future of composition in the Western mode lies in the adaptation and development of the native modes. Viscount Konoye has already shown what can be done in this direction, and progress along these lines might eventually lead to interesting results.

The craze for ballet that swept over England in the years between the two wars reached Japan some five or six years ago. It would really be kinder to pass over this matter in silence, for great as is the talent of the Japanese for imitation they cannot imitate the shape of our legs, and theirs are certainly not built for ballet dancing. Besides, they refuse to admit that even the technique of this art cannot be acquired unless training is commenced in infancy. Just before I left I attended a performance of *Les Sylphides*, which was followed by Debussy's *L'Après Midi d'un Faune*. It was greeted with rapturous applause; but in truth it might have been a burlesque such as we sometimes give in a revue. Young ladies with beer-bottle legs clattered about the stage and hovered uncertainly on their points; and as for the faun, it was only the hint of indecency in his movements that caused one to restrain one's laughter.

There is to me something pathetic in the slavish imitation of a foreign culture, but it was not until I saw the Japanese ballet that I realized what a pathetic nation this is. The performance was in some sense typical of the mental state of the younger generation, groping blindly for the Western culture that they believe will give them the answer to all life's problems, but which they can never really understand.

★ 22 ★

I HAD NOW BEEN IN TOKYO FOR JUST OVER THREE YEARS, AND DURING that time great changes had come about. I had arrived at the very moment when the effects of the China war were becoming perceptible; but now the deterioration was much more obvious, and very much more rapid. The city now presented a shabby appearance; not even the main streets were all repaired, so that on wet nights one had to splash through rain-filled potholes. The pavements, too, were badly in need of attention, but either there were no men to do the work or else the money was needed for other and more urgent purposes. The Ginza, which is Tokyo's chief thoroughfare, had formerly been ablaze with Neon Lights at night; now it was almost in darkness, for the current had to be conserved. In private houses the consumption of gas and electricity was severely rationed, the monthly allowance being barely sufficient for cooking. Imported foodstuffs, especially coffee, were difficult to come by, and while it was still possible to live in reasonable comfort, this now called for considerable ingenuity. Pure cotton and woollen goods had long since disappeared from the market, but at first this did not greatly affect foreign residents; it was still possible to import things from Shanghai.

Anti-spy posters appeared on every hoarding, and the people were warned against the activities of the ubiquitous fifth-column. This campaign was directed, of course, primarily against the British and Americans. The Germans were for the time being safe. But there is good reason to believe that their anti-Japanese activities are well known to the police, who will act in no uncertain way when the tide turns. The Germans themselves are well aware of this. Many of them, small business men and clerks for the most part, had been glad to supplement their earnings by working for their Embassy Gestapo. But when they saw British and American nationals being arrested on trumped-up charges of having engaged in espionage, they began to get apprehensive, especially when one or two of their own number were held and later sentenced. There was, however, no way of escape; once a man agrees to co-operate with the Gestapo he is in a trap; he cannot but go on until fate overtakes him.

As for me, the anti-spy campaign was little more than a nuisance. Small boys would come and chalk the word on my front door, and sometimes groups of them would shout it at me as I walked down the street, but always with a laugh. I doubt if they understood the meaning of the word. It was on one of these days, too, that I met with rude treatment (the only occasion this happened during the whole of my stay in Japan), when an army officer pushed me out of the way with his sword scabbard, swore, and shoved me into the muddy gutter. But I only laughed, which annoyed him more than ever.

Although the situation was getting worse it was apparently not yet critical. A certain number of British people, whose presence in the country was not absolutely necessary, had already been evacuated, but, while all of us were advised to go, it was thought that a few of the teachers who held key positions might still do useful work for the British cause by remaining a few more months. I decided to stay. I was extremely interested to see how the situation was going to develop, and I wanted to see things through to the end. There was also another factor, which the reader may find it difficult to comprehend; I had grown extremely fond of the Japanese people. But I do not wish this statement to be misinterpreted. The majority of my friends were intellectuals, many of whom would have done anything to prevent this war and were profoundly shocked when it came. That they had been, in point of fact, ineffectual is beside the point.

I desire most earnestly to see Japan's military might utterly destroyed. This, in my opinion, is necessary not only for the well-being of the world at large, but also for that of the Japanese people themselves. They cannot display themselves as they truly are while their country is ordered by its present band of military gangsters. It is true, of course, that they lack the courage to stand up for themselves as individuals, but it could hardly be otherwise in a people brought up for generation after generation to suppress every form of individuality. In normal times Japan is a pleasant country to live in; especially if one does not share the usual Anglo-Saxon prejudices and conventions, and is prepared to go at least some way through the looking glass.

AFTER PEARL HARBOUR

7th December 1941 to 29th July 1942

★ *1* ★

SUNDAY THE 7TH DECEMBER, 1941 WAS MUCH THE SAME AS ANY OTHER. I had got up rather late, played over a few records before lunch, and spent the afternoon writing an article on Virginia Woolf. It was never published and is now, I believe, in the archives of the Japanese police.

My article was for *Japan News Week*, the American paper that had somehow managed to keep its independence right up to the outbreak of war. Its acknowledged policy was to promote amicable relations between the United States and Japan. This it attempted to do by means of extremely outspoken leading articles, which criticized impartially the attitude of both countries. In the same spirit of impartiality it also published, in adjacent columns, two weekly summaries of the war situation in the exact form in which they were supplied by the British and German Embassies respectively. These, taken together, often formed amusing reading. As relations between Germany and Japan became closer, however, the German Embassy hinted at the desirability of editing the British summary in such a way that it should not contradict the official German news. This the editor flatly declined to do, upon which the German Embassy ceased to supply him with its own summary.

For some months before the outbreak of war three or four of us who were working for the paper had been accustomed to meet every Sunday night at the house of Paul Rusch, one of the best friends Japan has ever had. Paul had originally come to Japan as a voluntary Y.M.C.A. worker to help the Japanese after the terrible earthquake of 1933. He had later become an educational missionary and, in the course of years, had brought into being, almost entirely through his own efforts, what was probably one of the finest social service camps for boys in the world. This camp was well on the way towards

THE OUTBREAK OF WAR

completion when the war put an end to Paul's activities. He is also known as the introducer of American football into Japan.

Paul's dinners were much appreciated by all his guests. He had a high regard for the pleasures of the table, was an extremely skilled cook, and would often give us a dinner prepared and cooked entirely by himself. In these feasts, dishes peculiar to his own Kentucky would take a prominent place. Long after the rest of us had been forced by rationing difficulties to give up all forms of entertainment, Paul's hospitality continued. How he did it, we never found out, and it still remains his secret.

On the night of 7th December we had gathered, as usual, at Paul's home; W. R. Wills, the Editor of *Japan News Week*, Phyllis Argall, the managing Editor of the paper, Air-Commodore Bryant, the British Air Attaché, and myself. It was not often that we had a member of the diplomatic corps to give tone to our Sunday night parties. Besides, he brought other advantages. The petrol restriction, which had now made it almost impossible to get a taxi late at night, did not apply to members of the Embassy; when they went out to dinner they travelled in their own private cars, and it had become more or less understood that before returning to their own houses they should first see home any fellow-guests who did not share their privileges. As this happened to be an unusually wet night, we were delighted to see Bryant's saloon standing in front of Paul's door. There would, at any rate, be no need to rush away early; no standing in a dripping bus queue, no strap hanging on an overcrowded last suburban train. But, of course, we were glad to see Bryant for his own sake, and to hear the latest news from home. It was only when we happened to meet someone from the Embassy that we had a chance of hearing what was really happening; for, although it was in theory possible for Englishmen in Tokyo to go to the Embassy and collect a copy of the daily bulletin, in actual practice this was seldom done, as regular visits to the British Embassy placed even British subjects under grave police suspicion. In fact, after Japan entered the war a number of our nationals were arrested for the " offence " of having paid regular visits to their own embassy. The Japanese police were unwilling to believe that one might go there with no more dangerous object than to drink a cup of tea.

After dinner we all sat talking round the fire. Most of us had realized for some time that Japan's entry into the war was now inevitable, but no one thought the moment was yet at hand. I think if anyone had told us that, as we sat there enjoying our quiet chat, the Japanese fleet was already in position in front of Pearl Harbour, we should have laughed at the idea. No one had received any hint that

THE OUTBREAK OF WAR

the crisis had been reached. We left Paul's house at about eleven o'clock, and Bryant, after seeing Wills and Phyllis Argall home, took me on in the direction of my house which was not very far from his. As it was getting late and he had to be up early in the morning, I asked him to drop me at the cross-roads near his own house. There, accordingly, he stopped the car and we sat in it, smoking a last cigarette, before I got out and walked home. The streets were deserted; I cannot remember seeing a single soul on my way. And yet it later transpired that not only did the police know exactly who was dining at Paul's house that night, but that they had also kept an eye on Bryant and me talking in his car at the cross-roads. No doubt I was shadowed all the way to my house, but such is the efficiency of the Japanese police that I was totally unaware of it. During the whole of my four years' stay in Japan I cannot recall a single occasion when I so much as suspected that I was being watched, and yet reports which I subsequently received made it clear that the police had kept an eye on me the whole time.

On the following morning I came down to breakfast as usual at about half-past eight. At this hour there was a daily broadcast of gramophone records, and I generally listened to it as I ate my breakfast. I switched on the radio, but instead of hearing a symphony, I heard an announcer talking rapidly in Japanese. He seemed to be saying the same thing over and over again, so I thought I had better try and make out what it was all about. As far as I could understand, the announcer was saying that a state of war now existed between Japan and the United States. (The news of the actual attack on Pearl Harbour was not made public until about an hour later.) As I was not quite certain whether I had understood correctly, I called in my cook and asked her if the news was true. "Yes," she said, "but go on with your breakfast, or you'll be late for your work." I was uncertain what to do, so I thought first of all I would go and talk things over with Reuter's correspondent, Richard Tenelly, who was now my next-door neighbour. As soon as I had stepped out of my door, however, I noticed four or five policemen on guard outside Tenelly's. They told me their chief was inside and that I had better see him. He came down almost at once and I asked what I should do. "We have no orders to arrest you," he said, "so you had better carry on with your work as usual." I told him that I was due to give a lecture at ten, and he advised me to go away and deliver it. He refused to let me see Tenelly.

On arriving at the University I went straight to my class-room and set about delivering my lecture. There was nothing abnormal in the behaviour of the students and we carried on as though nothing had

THE OUTBREAK OF WAR

happened. At the end of the lecture, however, I was told that I had better do no further teaching pending the receipt of instructions from the Department of Education. In the meantime, it occurred to me that I would do well to visit the Foreign Office in order to find out exactly what my position now was. I have already explained that I originally went to Japan under the ægis of the Foreign Office, and although the matter was never committed to writing it was understood that in the event of war I should be afforded what practically amounted to diplomatic immunity. I found the office in a turmoil; indeed, the officials with whom I spoke seemed just as much surprised and stunned by the news as the ordinary man in the street. To-day it is widely believed that the sending of Mr. Kurusu to Washington with the ostensible purpose of making a last minute attempt to prevent war was one of the most underhand diplomatic actions ever committed, since the plans for attacking Pearl Harbour had already been made and the Japanese navy was actually moving into position while Mr. Kurusu's negotiations were still in progress.[1] It is doubtful if the whole truth will ever be known, but when I call to memory my conversations with members of the Japanese Foreign Office on the morning of 8th December I am inclined to believe that the Japanese Government acted in good faith. I think it is not unlikely that the attack on Pearl Harbour was launched by the Armed Forces without the previous sanction of the Government in Tokyo.[2] I am well aware that this opinion will not be generally acceptable, but it should be remembered that the Japanese army chiefs already had established

[1] On the 7th December 1941, the Japanese Ambassador, together with Mr. Kurusu, handed a document to the American Secretary of State, one hour *after* the Japanese had launched their attack on Pearl Harbour. A few minutes later the Secretary of State expressed himself to the Japanese Ambassador in the following terms:

"I must say that in all my conversations with you during the last nine months I have never uttered one word of untruth. This is borne out absolutely by the record. In all my fifty years of public service I have never seen a document that was more crowded with infamous falsehoods and distortions—infamous falsehoods and distortion on a scale so huge that I never imagined until to-day that any Government on this planet was capable of uttering them."

[2] Since writing the above I have discovered that I am not alone in this belief. Otto D. Tolischus, former *New York Times* correspondent in Japan, writes as follows of the events of 7th December, 1941 : " I didn't then know that President Roosevelt had sent a personal message to the Emperor with a last appeal for peace. It had been delayed in transmission, presumably purposely, and it was not till midnight that Grew [Mr. Joseph C. Grew, American Ambassador to Japan] was able to present it to Togo [Mr. Shiginori Togo, Japanese Foreign Minister]. As Grew later told me, he was convinced that Togo himself did not know then that war was at hand."—*Tokyo Record* (Hamish Hamilton, London, June 1943, page 223.)

JAPANESE POLICE METHODS

a precedent for taking independent action by their seizure of Manchuria in 1931 without obtaining the prior sanction of their Home Government.

I was told by the Foreign Office that orders had already been issued to the effect that I was not to be arrested. But it was added that I should be well advised to remain at home for the next few days, or at any rate until it was possible to see how the situation was developing. If I myself did not feel uneasy, however, there was no objection to my going out in the neighbourhood of my own home. Nevertheless, before going back to my house, I decided to visit my friend Frank Hawley, who was director of the British Library of Information and Culture, an institute which had recently been opened under the auspices of the British Council. It is remarkable that, in spite of the close relations we have maintained with Japan for many years, no one had apparently ever thought it worth while to establish such a library in the days of peace. A British institute could have had very considerable influence in increasing the already great interest in, and respect for, things English. In the event, the British Library was not opened until relations between the two countries had already become strained, and it came under the suspicions of the police from the start. But even during its short existence it did valuable work, many teachers and students taking advantage of the excellent selection of books which had been sent out from England by the British Council, although this often made them liable to police questioning.

When I arrived at Hawley's house I found that both he and his Japanese wife had been arrested early in the morning and taken to the local police station. His cook told me that she thought it would be unwise to make any attempt to get in touch with him; she herself, when taking food and bedding to her master and mistress, had been denied access to them.

★ 2 ★

IT WAS NOT UNTIL WE MET ON THE REPATRIATION SHIP, SOME EIGHT months later, that I heard Hawley's story. I am giving it here in some detail because it throws considerable light on Japanese police methods and prison administration.

Before doing so, however, it will be well to explain briefly the constitution of the Japanese Police. In Japan there are two distinct police forces, the ordinary civil police and the military security police. The duties of the civil police are not confined to the maintenance of public order. They keep a strict control over what has come to be known as "dangerous thought," a convenient expression which covers every form of activity in any way opposed to the traditional Japanese way of thinking. One of their chief concerns is the eradication of communism.

The military police constitutes a definite branch of the army; but unlike the military police in most other countries, it is a body with a policy of its own. It stands for the extreme of reactionary nationalism. Of its two main functions, the preservation of discipline in the army takes the less important place. The members of the force who are engaged in this minor branch of its activity have duties exactly similar to those of our own "Red Caps." They wear ordinary military uniform with the addition of a white brassard on which is written the ideographs for *Kempei*, meaning "Military Police."

The chief function of the military security police is the protection of the country in a very wide sense. It includes the prevention of espionage and the carrying out of extensive counter-espionage activities. This force is in many ways the counterpart of the German *Gestapo*, but it should be noted that its members, although they hold military rank, seldom wear any sort of uniform. No civil policeman can arrest a member of the armed forces, but the military police are vested with authority to arrest anybody; in fact most of those who incur their displeasure are civilians. In this connection it should also be noted that every police station in Japan has a member of the military police attached to it as a liaison officer. In theory, the two forces work in close co-operation with each other, but actually there is considerable jealousy between them. This makes for certain weaknesses; for it sometimes happens that a man is arrested by the civil police and discharged because on examination it cannot be proved that he has contravened any of the regulations for the upholding of which they are responsible. Had the same man been arrested by the military police, it would probably have been found possible to prove a charge against him.

Hawley and his wife were arrested by the civil police at six-thirty on the morning of the 8th December, 1941, on a charge of having contravened the National Mobilization Law. This law, which had only recently come into operation, has so wide a net that in theory practically everyone in Japan renders himself liable to arrest; it embraces, for instance, such apparently harmless activities as being in possession of a complete file of newspapers, or discussing in public

JAPANESE POLICE METHODS

the Japanese war news that appears in the daily papers. Several of my own students were in fact later arrested because a policeman had overheard them harmlessly discussing the American air raid on Tokyo when they were on their way to school in a tram.

On arrival at the local police station, Hawley and his wife were immediately separated. He was made to empty his pockets and hand over his tie and braces, after which the two of them were conducted to underground cells. Later on, they were put into cages measuring about five feet square. They each had one of these cages to themselves; but ordinary Japanese prisoners are confined four in a cage and are required to squat all day in the correct ceremonial fashion, that is to say with the feet tucked underneath the body. It should be remembered that even a Japanese who is accustomed to squat on the floor cannot remain in the strict ceremonial posture for more than half an hour at most without suffering extreme discomfort. Hawley told me that he saw a number of Japanese youths who, to judge by the growth of their beards, seemed to have been confined in these cages for several months. For during this preliminary stage of detention no shaving is permitted; nor are the prisoners allowed any form of exercise. Moreover, no matter what the physical state of the prisoner, he is only given the opportunity to relieve himself once in every six hours. The conveniences, Hawley told me, were indescribably filthy. The use of toilet paper was not permitted; there was one cold water tap, but no towels. The food was one bowl of rice with a small quantity of vegetables three times a day.

After thirteen hours Hawley and his wife were removed to a detention prison (at Sugamo, in the suburbs of Tokyo), which is considered by the Japanese to be a model of its kind. It was in this prison that most of the foreigners who were arrested in Tokyo were confined. On arrival Hawley was told to strip; he was then measured and weighed, but there was no medical examination. Next, he had to stand naked while a prison official made a diagrammatic sketch of his body both from behind and from the front. This showed the exact position of every distinguishing feature. The two diagrams were then pasted on to a card about six inches square, on the back of which full details regarding hair, teeth, etc., were entered. This card accompanies the prisoner whenever he goes outside the gaol, the idea being that should he escape, the warder in charge can hand it in immediately to the nearest police station for identification purposes. The preparation of these diagrams took about three hours, during the whole of which time Hawley was naked except for a thin cotton kimono, which he was constantly called upon to remove.

Then followed a compulsory bath which, including undressing and dressing, he was required to complete within seven minutes. This is the standard time allowed for bathing in all Japanese prisons. Hawley was permitted to retain his own clothes. No necktie was allowed him, but he was left his braces during the day, surrendering them every evening before his cell was locked for the night. Japanese prisoners, it may be noted, are not permitted to wear any sort of foreign clothing; they must wear some form of national dress.

After the compulsory bath Hawley was taken to his cell, carrying his first meal with him. The cell was six feet by nine and had a cement floor covered with thin Japanese matting. It contained a small cupboard, flush toilet, and a wash basin fitted with a cold water tap. There was no furniture, the only alternative to squatting on the floor being to sit on the lavatory seat. There was in addition a twig brush for cleaning the cell, a paper dustpan and a wooden waste-paper basket into which the dust from the floor was emptied; it was removed once every week. There was one barred window two feet by four; it was of opaque glass covered with wire netting, hinged at the top and so arranged that it could not be opened for more than six inches. There was no heating of any kind in the winter and the cell was stifling in summer. One 30-watt bulb hung from the centre of the ceiling; this was kept burning throughout the night, and since all prisoners are required to sleep in such a way that their faces can be seen by the duty warder on his rounds, it is impossible to avoid the glare of the unshaded lamp. The door of the cell was of steel, with an observation hole three inches in diameter. This hole was closed during the day but kept open throughout the night.

Such were the conditions, with little variation, in which all foreigners who were arrested in Tokyo had to live, and in some other places they seem to have been markedly worse. But it is important to note that judged by Japanese standards the conditions imposed were good, for there is no doubt whatsoever that the treatment accorded to Japanese prisoners is considerably more harsh. The press, however, both in this country and in America, has commented indignantly on the barbarous way in which foreigners were treated. It is perfectly true that in many cases they were roughly handled; but not, I think, because they were foreigners. There was not, generally speaking, any discrimination against foreigners as such; they were, as I have said, rather better treated on the whole than Japanese in similar circumstances would have been. What is wrong is the whole Japanese judicial system; in favour of that there is nothing to be said.

Here is a brief account of the prison life of all those awaiting trial.

Prisoners are required to get up at seven o'clock in summer and at six in winter. Thirty minutes later each cell is opened and inspected

JAPANESE POLICE METHODS

by the chief warder. Half an hour later breakfast is brought, consisting of a mixture of boiled rice and wheat, or barley, with the addition of a small quantity of vegetable soup. There is a prison shop where those awaiting trial may buy extra food, soap, tooth paste, toilet paper, and similar odds and ends. Foreign prisoners are allowed to have ordinary European food prepared in the gaol. They are not required to live on Japanese food. Should they receive a sentence, however, they are then treated in the same way as ordinary Japanese prisoners.

Prisoners are not permitted to shave themselves but are allowed to visit the barber's shop every four days or so.

On fine days prisoners are allowed to exercise for ten minutes at ten o'clock every morning. The exercise takes place in outdoor cells measuring twenty-five feet by six. These cells have walls but no roof, and were described to me as being like chicken-runs. Whenever a prisoner leaves his cell he is required to cover his head with a large basket, in shape something like a waste-paper basket. The object of this is to prevent prisoners recognizing each other. The basket is even worn in the streets when, for instance, a prisoner is being taken from the gaol to the building in which his examination takes place.

At eleven o'clock there is a general inspection of cells, and while it is in progress each prisoner waits outside his cell with his basket on his head.

Lunch is served at eleven-thirty and is the same as breakfast with the addition of a little fish. The evening meal, again the same, comes at four in the afternoon. At half-past four there is another inspection similar to that which takes place in the morning, and at five o'clock the prisoner is locked into his cell for the night. During the daytime the cell-door can be opened from the outside without a key, but after the evening inspection the door is locked. Bedtime is at seven in both summer and winter, but there appears to be no objection to a prisoner staying up till eight o'clock. By this hour, however, all prisoners must be actually in bed.

Prisoners awaiting trial are allowed to have six books a month. These must be in mint condition, and are censored by the prison authorities before being handed over. As the censoring takes at least one month, the prisoner is without reading matter of any kind during his first four weeks of detention.

Every prisoner is allowed to write one post card every ten days and may receive any letters which the authorities consider suitable. In order to write, however, the prisoner is taken to a special cell which is not more than two and a half feet square ! Yes, I mean what I say: two and a half feet square. Writing material is provided, but nothing may be taken into the writing cell; not even toilet paper or a handkerchief. No time limit is imposed for the writing of the post card. It should be realized, however, that the cell is so small that it is impossible even to turn round in it. In summer the heat is so great that only a man of exceptional physique is able to remain in the writing cell for more than a few minutes.

After a prisoner has been sentenced the conditions become very markedly worse. Only prison clothing is allowed, consisting of one thin cotton kimono in summer, and a slightly thicker one in winter. Underclothing is not permitted. The kimonos issued to those who are in prison for minor offences are blue, and those given to men under sentence for major crimes are blood-red. The head is kept closely shaved; the chin receives attention once a month. Prisoners under sentence must rise thirty minutes earlier in the morning than those awaiting trial, and go to bed one hour later in the evening. They are required to work, for the most part in solitary confinement, from the time of rising in the morning until their cells are locked up for the night. Work consists in making match-boxes, cardboard boxes, simple toys, envelopes, and stitching already cut garments for prison use. All tools, needles, and so on must be surrendered before bed time.

Bedding, in the case of all prisoners, is confined to two Japanese quilts; one to lie on and one with which to cover oneself. Those awaiting trial, however, may have extra bedding sent in from their homes. One pillow is provided. This is shaped like a sausage, about eight inches long and four inches thick. It is stuffed with rice husks.

A bath is allowed once in every five days, no matter whether the prisoner has been sentenced or is only awaiting trial. This, like the compulsory bath on first entering the prison, must be completed within seven minutes.

Once a prisoner has been sentenced he must live entirely on the food provided by the prison authorities. He is not in any circumstances allowed to buy any extra food from the prison shop; nor may he write or receive letters during the first year of his sentence.

★ 3 ★

AS A RESULT OF HIS EXPERIENCES DURING SOME EIGHT MONTHS CONfinement in Sugamo prison, Hawley told me that he considered that it would be only fair to describe the actual prison authorities as humane. So far as the regulations permitted, they did what they could to make the life of their charges bearable; but what he had to say concerning the Judicial Police is quite another matter. At the risk of holding up my story I must find place here for an outline of Japanese criminal procedure. To the best of my belief my account is the first of its kind, partly, no doubt, because before this war no foreigner had had actual experience of the inside of a Japanese gaol; and no Japanese could, of course, describe these matters without rendering him liable to further imprisonment. A great deal of the information which follows would, I imagine, be new even to the vast majority of the inhabitants of Japan.

Before the police can make an arrest they must first obtain the permission of the Board of Procurators, who issue the necessary warrant. The Procurators, however, will not issue a warrant unless the police are able to convince them that they have good grounds for suspicion.

When the warrant has been issued the actual arrest is made by a group of plain-clothes policemen, members of what is known as the "Special Section." The law requires that the warrant authorizing arrest be shown to the accused person upon his request. But apparently this is not always done. At any rate, one or two foreigners who were arrested in connection with the present war did, to my certain knowledge, ask that the warrant should be produced, and in each case this was refused.

After arrest, the accused person may be confined either in a police station or in a detention prison. This explains how it came about that some of the prisoners seen by Hawley at his local police station had by all appearances already been there for several months.

Japanese warrants of arrest are couched in extremely vague terms. They authorize arrest in order that the appropriate authorities may have an opportunity of investigating whether there is suspicion that the accused person has infringed such and such a law. It is not necessary that they should contain a specified charge.

According to Japanese law, examination must be begun within two months of arrest. At the end of this period, the police, who themselves conduct the preparatory examination, are required to report to the Procurator's office whether, in their opinion, there are, or are not, grounds for suspicion. Nevertheless, several Dutch nationals, arrested in December, 1941, were held without examination until March in the following year.

The system of detention for the purpose of investigation is technically known as " Prohibition of Intercourse." During the first two months the accused person may not see anybody, other than prison or police officials, without the permission of the Board of Procurators. In actual practice this permission is never granted.

At the end of two months, if in the opinion of the police there is no suspicion of guilt, the Board of Procurators will order the accused to be released. Release must, however, be specifically recommended by the police. In practice this is seldom done since the number of days during which a person may be held without being handed over for trial, either in a public court or by a preliminary judge, is fixed by law at one hundred and twenty days, and the police are generally unwilling to come to a decision before the expiry of this period.

In the case of persons suspected of being communists the period of permissible detention for examination is increased to three hundred and sixty-five days.

No permission is necessary in order to detain a suspected person for the first sixty days; but on the sixty-first day it is necessary for the Procurator's office to inform the suspected person that good reason has been found for detaining him for a further thirty days. These notices must be renewed monthly until the accused is handed over for public trial.

If the police do not advise the Procurators that the suspect should be released, he will almost certainly be detained for at least a further two months. The reason for this is that if the police have even the slightest suspicion against the accused the Procurators are compelled to investigate the matter.

An accused person in detention has no possibility of communicating with the outside world until the Procurators have decided, as a result of the preliminary police investigation, that he is guilty. That is to say, his first interview, even with his lawyer, cannot take place until the expiry of the first hundred and twenty days. It should be noted that, according to Japanese law, an accused person is held guilty until he is able to prove his innocence. This is exactly the reverse of British law, according to which the accused is held to be innocent until his guilt is proved.

The Procurator is not required to give an accused person any information other than the plain fact that in his opinion he has infringed such and such a law. He is not told in what way he has transgressed.

Here are some further notes on the methods adopted by the Japanese police in their examination of accused persons. They are compiled from the actual experiences of various British nationals who were arrested in December, 1941.

The accused has no right to ask questions of his examiner but, on the the other hand, he may be interrogated as much as his examiners wish. He has not the right to demand proof of any statement made by his examiners, nor to see any written evidence stated to be held against him. He is not permitted to see any other prisoner, even in cases where the prisoner in question has made a confession, the contents of which have a bearing on his own case.

An accused person may be examined at any time between eight in the morning and three the following morning; there is no actual fixed period. One of my friends was subjected to continous examination from nine o'clock in the morning until half-past ten at night, during the course of which he fainted from sheer exhaustion. During the whole of this time he was allowed only one interval of thirty minutes for lunch. There was no break for the evening meal. Another acquaintance was stripped, made to kneel in front of his examiners, beaten with the flat of a Japanese sword, and threatened with mutilation if he refused to confess. All prisoners were constantly shouted at and threatened with penal servitude for ten years, to be reduced to five years if they made a confession. It should be noted, however, that in the majority of cases the accused persons were not even told the specific nature of the charge against them; they were merely urged to confess to having contravened the regulations. Needless to say, none did so.

The examiners have the usual portable Japanese fire bowls beside them, but the prisoner has no heating of any kind. He is made to sit on a small hard chair and is not allowed to move about; he may not even rise to ease his limbs from cramp. One man was nearly blinded by having a hundred-watt lamp constantly shining in his eyes throughout the examination.

The examination is conducted by only one man, who is a member of the Judicial Police. A witness, also a member of the police, is present in order to see that the examination is conducted fairly, but it appears that the witness constantly takes sides with the examiner, and in at least one case known to me he took part in the examiner's attack on a prisoner.

The examination of foreign prisoners is conducted through an interpreter, unless their knowledge of the Japanese language makes this unnecessary. I know of only one foreigner who was able to dispense with an interpreter.

It seems that during the first month of examination the prisoner's answers to questions are not carefully recorded. Later on, when the whole examination is committed to writing, the prisoner's replies are not infrequently altered so as to reverse the sense of the words he actually used. The average prisoner has no means of checking what is written down. Even if he has a fairly good knowledge of the spoken language, he is very unlikely to have any but the most elementary knowledge of the Japanese script. The one and only informant known to me who had a real knowledge of Japanese told me that he frequently had to protest that his replies were being incorrectly recorded. Every dossier has to be signed by the accused on the last page. Most prisoners, however, have no idea what they are signing, and are obliged to take the interpreter's word that the written evidence is a correct record of what has been said. The pages are not numbered.

The whole purpose of the police examination is to try and secure a confession, as without this an accused person cannot be convicted. The method adopted in the case of most of the foreigners arrested on the outbreak of the war was to play off one against another; thus, the examination would be broken off to tell an accused that so-and-so had just made a full confession in which he was implicated, and that he himself would therefore do well to confess. Incidentally, it is of interest to note that the only persons to be tried by a jury are those who deny all the evidence against them. In actual practice, however, Japanese juries are completely subservient to the judge. This means that it is not to the prisoner's advantage to be tried by jury.

The technique followed in the Procurator's examination is the same as that used by the Police. An attempt is made, however, to discredit what the prisoner said in his police examination, and thus involve him in a major contradiction. On the conclusion of the Procurator's examination the prisoner may be dismissed as innocent, or may be released under the terms of a clause meaning, in translation, " Suspension of Proceedings." This means that the Procurator considers the prisoner guilty, but is prepared to suspend proceedings. Such cases, however, are extremely rare.

If the suspicion of guilt is so great that the Procurator feels certain that he can secure a conviction by public trial, he hands the prisoner over to the local or district criminal court. If, however, he is uncertain, he hands the accused over for examination by a Preliminary Judge.

The function of a Preliminary Judge is to determine whether or not the Procurator's belief in the prisoner's guilt is justified. When he has

JAPANESE CRIMINAL PROCEDURE

satisfied himself that it is, he hands the prisoner over to the appropriate court; otherwise he dismisses him. It should be noted, however, that the Preliminary Judge usually takes not less than six months, and very often several years, before he decides whether the suspicion of guilt is sufficient or not to secure conviction.

During the whole of this period the prisoner is not allowed under Japanese law to consult a lawyer regarding his case. He may, however, with the express permission of the judge, be visited by a lawyer in the presence of witnesses, but he is only allowed to discuss personal matters such as the disposal of his property. He may not, for instance, make a will. During this period the prisoner may, in theory, receive visits of five minutes' duration from his relatives once a month, but in actual practice the judge often refuses permission.

At the beginning of the examination by the Preliminary Judge the Procurator's statement to the accused is read out to him. This is a summary of the evidence which is considered incriminating.

Prisoners may apply in writing from the prison for examination by the Preliminary Judge. In such cases the Judge is compelled to call the prisoner to his court within one month of receipt of the application. In actual practice, however, the judge merely examines the prisoner for ten minutes or so and sends him back to prison. One of my friends, thinking it would hasten matters, made the necessary request for examination by the Preliminary Judge. He was left in a small underground cell beneath the court for twelve hours, after which he was called up and asked a few vague questions. He said that he was glad to return to the comparative comfort of his prison cell. Moreover, the same friend told me that when in due course he came up before the Preliminary Judge in the ordinary course of events, the Judge made no attempt to elicit the truth; he merely accepted the statements of the police and Procurator as true.

Even after the police and Procurator's examinations have been concluded it is often several months before the prisoner is brought to trial. It can thus be seen that even when an accused is acquitted, as was the case with the majority of the British and American nationals arrested in December, 1941, he has served what is to all intents and purposes a prison sentence extending in some cases to as long as a year. Japanese law is so constituted, moreover, that it enables an accused person, even when there is not the faintest shadow of evidence against him, to be held in custody almost indefinitely. Nearly all my friends and acquaintances who were arrested were eventually discharged without a stain on their characters. They had been imprisoned for various periods up to eight months, but no compensation for wrongful arrest was offered them. Japanese law does not, indeed, recognize the rights of the accused; or, if it recognizes them, is applied in such a way that it is better for an accused person not to claim his privileges.

In conclusion, here are a few additional notes on the procedure adopted by judges in Japan.

The Procurator's statement to the Preliminary Judge is read out at the beginning of the latter's examination. No comment is made upon it. This is followed by the judge's examination, at the end of which he merely informs the prisoner whether in his opinion there is sufficient evidence against him to justify his being handed over to the courts for trial. Once the prisoner has been so informed, he is, at any rate in theory, free to have interviews in prison both with his friends and with his lawyer. This freedom of consultation is, however, illusory. In the Sugamo detention prison, for instance, the opportunities for having interviews were limited by the fact that the prison contains only twenty cubicles in which prisoners may hold interviews. During the period in which my friends were incarcerated there were some twelve hundred prisoners awaiting trial. In order to obtain the use of a cubicle one had to spend some hours waiting in a queue, so that in actual practice a prisoner was unable to see his lawyer for more than three or four periods of one hour and a half each. The interviews took place in the presence of police witnesses, who made a record of every word spoken and handed it over to the judge. All conversations had to be carried on in Japanese, but if the prisoner's knowledge of this language was insufficient he had to converse through an interpreter; he was not allowed to communicate direct in English or any language other than Japanese.

It appears that during the trial the defending lawyer is not permitted to dispute the prisoner's guilt. All he can do is to set forth extenuating circumstances. Nor is the prisoner allowed to call witnesses in his defence, should the Procurator and Judge decide, after consultation, that it is not in the interest of the state to permit him to do so.

For reasons which I have already explained, trial by jury is not usual. In serious cases there are three judges; otherwise, only one. The trial generally lasts for one day, but the verdict is not given until two or three weeks later.

Although they are called public trials, the majority of trials in the Japanese courts are held *in camera*. The defending lawyer may not put questions to the Procurator, and can only address the prisoner when special permission is given. He is not allowed to cross-examine the witnesses for the prosecution.

In conclusion, I may say that I am not competent to compare the legal system of Japan with that of other countries, or to make a learned commentary on it. But speaking as a layman, it seems to me obvious that the dice are so heavily loaded against any person unfortunate enough to fall into the clutches of the Japanese police that, if they make up their minds to secure a conviction, the question of his innocence does not even arise. It may be that Japanese law as codified is reasonably humane. But as it is applied it would appear to be little better than a travesty.

★ 4 ★

I MUST NOW RETURN TO MY OWN STORY. FINDING THAT THERE WAS nothing I could do to help the Hawleys I went back to my own house. I found about eight policemen there. Everything was in disorder; my books were lying all over the floor, my clothes had been pulled out of the cupboards, the bedding was heaped in the middle of the room. And then they questioned me. " Had I a short-wave transmitter concealed in the house ? Had I perhaps a machine-gun, or at any rate a rifle ? " No; I had none of these things; but not until they had made a thorough search of every nook and corner were they satisfied. They went through all my letters, examined my photographs and took away with them a series of large X-ray negatives of my lungs. These I had kept by me for many years for the purpose of periodical comparisons. I never got them back. I was quite unable to convince the inspector that they were not in reality photographs of secret fortifications. They also selected for removal some half-dozen of my books, all of them with red bindings, since in the minds of the Japanese police books in red covers are thought to be connected in some way with communism. To these were added a very large pile of newspapers, some a year old. Fortunately for me, these papers were not consecutive, for, although I did not then know it, it had recently become a penal offence to possess a consecutive file of newspapers. Soon after the police departed, one of my students dropped in to see if I was all right. " I've just seen a most extraordinary sight," he said. " Oh," I replied, " what was it ? " He then went on to describe how, as he was walking up to my house, he had passed a squad of policemen, each one staggering along under a weight of English newspapers.

After this preliminary investigation I was left more or less alone for a few days. Then the police again visited me. It appeared that they were not completely satisfied that the contents of my library were harmless and wanted to examine my books in greater detail. I wondered how they were going to do this because it soon became apparent

RATIONING

that none of them knew any English. They were expecting me to explain the contents of each one of my books to them. But when my patience (to say nothing of my Japanese) proved unequal to this task, they contented themselves with looking at the pictures in such books as were illustrated. When they were doing this I suddenly noticed a large pile of pamphlets on the top of one of the shelves. These pamphlets had been sent out by the British Embassy to most of our nationals, the idea being that any Japanese guest who happened to come to one's house should be offered one. Most of them concerned the British war effort and were completely harmless; but (as many people were later to find out) their distribution was considered a sufficient excuse for arrest. Without saying anything, I picked up the bundle of pamphlets and quietly carried them into the lavatory, where I was able to dispose of them.

★ 5 ★

FOR THE FIRST FEW DAYS THERE WAS AN AIR OF BEWILDERMENT ABOUT the people; nobody seemed quite to believe that Japan had actually entered the war. This feeling was heightened by the fact that, except for the blackout, conditions remained much the same as they had been, and after the first week even the blackout was reduced to no more than a partial dimming of lights.

Petrol for civilian purposes had been getting short for some time past; now it was practically unobtainable. Taxis almost disappeared from the streets for a while. They were being converted to run on charcoal. The buses, too, were given similar treatment, with the result that the service, which hitherto had been fairly efficient, rapidly deteriorated. Even high Japanese officials were forced to use charcoal-burning cars, the only petrol-driven ones now on the streets being those belonging to the various embassies and legations.

A system of rationing was introduced immediately. Books were issued to every householder, but the actual distribution of food was made by the "Neighbourhood Association" of the street in which one lived. These Neighbourhood Associations, which had been started a few years ago, had come to play an important part in Japanese social life. Their organization was based on the old village associations, to which the Japanese had long been accustomed. With the growth of modern cities they had tended to disappear, but the Japanese,

RATIONING

who have a strongly developed sense of community life, had revived them in a modern form. The associations provided a practical way of dealing with some of the unusual conditions produced by the war with China. And now they were given the responsibility of administering the rationing system, and the local A.R.P. organization. As a householder I was, of course, a member of my local association, but I never attended any of its meetings, and had I done so it would, I imagine, have cause considerable embarrassment. My cook, however, used sometimes to attend on my behalf. She was, in fact, called to attend a special meeting very soon after the outbreak of war, the purpose of which was to discuss what precautions should be taken to deal with any foreign spies who might happen to be living in our street. Being at that time the only foreigner still at large, I took a personal interest in the outcome of these deliberations.

Not all rationed articles were distributed; some things such as meat, fish, vegetables, and fruit had to be fetched direct from the shops. This usually entailed waiting many hours in a queue, and if one was at the end of the line one often found nothing left to buy. Everybody was in theory entitled to a certain amount of meat and fish every week, but quite often none at all was on sale in the shops. This led to the report that even at the start of the war Japan was short of food. But actually there was no real food shortage; Japan grows sufficient rice to meet all her needs, and has an abundant supply of fish in home waters. Nobody likes living on an unchanging diet of fish and rice, but it should be realized that the Japanese have something of a genius for austerity. It is the consequence, perhaps, of an age-long training, and of having in the past been forced by their rulers to live in accordance with sumptuary laws, so that they can be called upon by their government to subsist for long periods on a diet so frugal that no European people would put up with it. That there appeared to be a shortage of food in Japan was due to various causes. In the first place, the extremely rigid price control, which was imposed immediately upon the outbreak of war, made farmers unwilling to send their produce into the cities. Lack of road transport, the result of petrol restrictions, was another important factor. Lack of petrol also accounted for the shortage of fish, for most of the fishing boats were petrol driven. Certain imported foodstuffs of course disappeared completely from the market. Chief among these was coffee, of which the Japanese are extremely fond. Its place was taken by a revolting *ersatz* liquid, made, I believe, from soya beans. Foreign wines and spirits also were difficult to obtain, although at the time I left Japan it was still possible to get hold of an occasional bottle of imported whisky. The price had risen to about £8; such luxuries were only obtainable on the black market. There seemed, however, to be plenty of Japanese who were willing and able to pay this exorbitant price.

When I got back to England one of the things that struck me most was the abundance of food. For months past I had been reading in the Japanese press about the terrible food shortage in England, so that it came as almost a shock, though an exceedingly pleasant one, to find how well we were being rationed. For the first few days the sight of well-stocked shops continued to amaze me. As for the cakes, I thought at first they must be dummies. Even before Japan came into the war, tinned foods were becoming difficult to obtain, and at the time I left most of the cake shops were closing down for lack of supplies.

I have often wondered whether the ordinary citizen in a free country realizes how immense is the influence of skilful propaganda. So constantly had I read that the people of Britain were rapidly approaching semi-starvation that in the end I had almost come to believe it. The little news about war conditions in England that was issued in Japan came almost entirely from German controlled sources, and there is no doubt that most Japanese believe that the situation here is desperate. Many of my friends, in fact, urged me to stay in Japan rather than risk starvation in England. Here is a particularly good example of the absurd length to which the Japanese press goes in its efforts to show that there is a grave food shortage in all parts of the British Empire. A message cabled from Lisbon by a staff correspondent of the *Tokyo Nichi Nichi* appeared in the issue of 5th March, 1942, as follows: " According to a report from Melbourne, the Australian Government to-day announced that Wiener sausages in Australia will soon be forced to change their shape. American sausage casings are no longer available and thus Australian butchers will have to wrap their sausages in the skins of sheep entrails rather than pigs' intestines, causing the shape of sausages to become longer and thinner."

One of the effects of the rationing system was to cause those who could afford it to make an even more frequent use of restaurants. In these the price was controlled, as it is in England, the maximum price for luncheon being fixed at three yen (about four shillings and sixpence), and for dinner at four yen; a cup of substitute coffee was included at both meals. No attempt was made to limit the number of dishes; in fact the number of courses remained much the same as it was before the war. But the quality rapidly deteriorated. Beef, which in normal times is both plentiful and excellent in Japan, practically disappeared, its place on the menu being taken more often than not by whale meat, an edible, but, to me at least, unpalatable substitute. But quite often there would be no meat of any sort available, even in the better restaurants, for days at a time. Many of these places had made extensive use of the black market at the beginning of the war and this had been discovered by the police, who, in revenge, now made it difficult for them to obtain even the supplies to which they were legally entitled.

One curious result of the run on the restaurants was that their patrons took their meals earlier and earlier, for unless one arrived at a restaurant betimes one found nothing left to eat. In ordinary times no eating-house ever closed before midnight; now they were shutting down by nine at the very latest. In order to make sure of obtaining a meal, people would arrive for lunch at eleven in the morning, and during my last few weeks in Japan I found it was necessary to arrive not later than five-thirty in the evening if I wanted to be sure of getting dinner. In fact, there would often be very little left to eat even at this hour. It was becoming quite usual for people to dine at three o'clock in the afternoon.

The food regulations were, I should say, fairly strictly regarded in the foreign-style restaurants in Tokyo. This was probably due to the fact that they were regularly patronized by the many non-Japanese residents still at large, to whom the police wished to give the necessary feeling of austerity. In the purely Japanese restaurants, however, it was quite otherwise. I have already explained that in these places one does not eat in public, but always in a private room. It is therefore easier to evade the regulations. The most common method of doing so was to order a meal for double the number of guests one was intending to entertain. This was, of course, expensive, but one was sure of getting an ample supply of food. To all bills in excess of the maximum price allowed to each person a government tax of an additional ten per cent was added; one had thus to pay this tax whenever one entertained, unless, as was frequently done, one asked for two separate bills and handed over to one's guest the cash to pay his own.

Up to the date of my departure from Japan, it was still possible to obtain most things in the way of foodstuffs on the black market, in spite of the fact that the present rationing system is an integral part of of the new National Mobilization laws, any infringement of which is punishable by a sentence of " more than one year " (in practice it usually means eighteen months) penal servitude. Many thousands of persons were already serving sentences for black market offences and a proposal was on foot to increase the penalty to one of " more than five years " penal servitude. Whether the increased penalty has yet been introduced I do not know, but *The Evening Standard* of the 3rd April, 1943 reported that fifteen persons had been sentenced to death in Tokyo for attempting to evade the food regulations.

There are in Tokyo large numbers of beer-halls, which are much frequented by young men of the student class. In normal times these are open at all hours of the day and do not close before midnight. Japanese beer, for the manufacture of which hops used to be imported, is a very pleasant light drink of the lager variety, and one could spend a pleasantly idle evening chatting in one of these places, particularly in the summer, when the city is less crowded. Very shortly after Japan entered the war, the supplies of beer became so restricted that the beer-halls were forced by the government to remain closed during the day. They opened only at five o'clock, by which hour there would be a queue (often a couple of hundred yards long) in front of each. Many of them were completely sold out by seven, and the majority closed their doors, for lack of supplies, at nine. Even in peacetime one would always find, as was only to be expected in such places, a certain number of people who had imbibed rather more than they could carry. The Japanese are quickly affected by alcohol, more quickly even than I am. I found that at the end of one evening, during which I consumed perhaps four or five small bottles of weak beer, I was not even elated, whereas I noticed that many Japanese would become completely drunk after consuming half the quantity. This is strange in view of the fact that as a nation the Japanese are extremely fond of all forms of alcohol. During the first few months following the outbreak of the war there was very much more drunkenness than before; so much of it in fact that I had to give up visiting beer-halls. In such places I was, of course, assumed to be a German, and it was embarrassing to be talked to by drunken strangers who took it for granted that one was rejoicing at the British reverses in the Far East. Whether the increase in drunkenness was due to over-indulgence caused by a psychological reaction to the war, or whether it was the chemical substitute used in place of hops I am unable to say. A Japanese medical friend told me that after the first few months of war there was a very noticeable increase in the number of patients admitted to the hospitals with stomach complaints of various kinds. Statistics were not forthcoming, but it appeared that most of these patients were regular beer drinkers.

In addition to the beer halls, there are literally thousands of small "dives" in Tokyo where drinks of various kinds can be obtained. Even in peacetime the quality of the liquor supplied in the more disreputable of these places was extremely suspect; the fact that your whisky was poured out of a genuine Haig bottle, with its seals intact, was no guarantee that the contents emanated from Scotland. The Japanese do, in fact, manufacture a whisky which is reasonably good; but the wartime stuff sold in most of these smaller drinking-dens was nothing less than methyl-alcohol. One of my own students drank a couple of glasses of this poison, and then, as he himself described it, felt as though he had been hit on the head with a mallet. He was seriously ill for

AIR RAID PRECAUTIONS: THE AMERICAN AIR RAID

several days and did not recover the full use of his mind for several weeks. This sort of thing, which is likely to increase as the war goes on, to say nothing of the bad, unnourishing food on which most Japanese are now forced to live, is bound in course of time to undermine the health of the rising generation.

★ 6 ★

EVEN BEFORE THE WAR SOME ATTEMPTS HAD BEEN MADE TO ORGANIZE air raid precautions in Japan. Elaborate displays had been held about twice a year in order to give those taking part a chance of demonstrating their efficiency; but no one took these affairs very seriously.

While the Neighbourhood Association had the duty of organizing A.R.P. locally, there was a Central Bureau which issued general instructions. The way in which these were interpreted often varied from street to street, depending upon the fancy of the president of the Neighbourhood Association concerned. Up to the time I left there was not, as there is in England, any full-time civil defence organization.

Every householder was required to keep a bucket of water on his doorstep, together with three or four small sacks filled with sand. These were intended for use in putting out fires, but actually they would have been quite ineffectual. The provision of ladders for each individual house was optional, so long as a certain number were available in every street. The women of every household were required to equip themselves with the Japanese equivalent of " slacks," loose baggy trousers worn over the ordinary kimono, and to don them immediately the alert was sounded. At this time, too, one member of the household, preferably the master himself, was supposed to stand on duty at the front door, there to await further instructions.

It might have been expected that in a city like Tokyo, where the majority of the houses are built of wood, a more efficient system of air raid precautions would have been instituted. That no serious effort has been made is, I believe, due to the fact that the greater part of the city is so inflammable that it is not humanly possible to protect it. The authorities are doubtless well aware that the present system has but a psychological value. They count on its reassuring the populace, and mitigating the panic which any large-scale raid is bound to cause.

To the best of my belief there are no air raid shelters in Tokyo, except in the Emperor's Palace and the German Embassy. An underground railway does indeed exist, but it runs too near the surface for the stations to afford protection against even moderately heavy bombs. Its stations, moreover, would afford protection for only a few thousand people. It seems doubtful if any attempt will be made to remedy this state of affairs. Tokyo is not like London, where there are many solid buildings which afford reasonable protection against all but a direct hit. To protect the people of Tokyo adequately would mean providing shelters for the entire population of the city, that is to say for between six and seven million people, and this is not a practicable proposition.

Until quite recently it was thought unlikely that Japan's enemies could ever secure bases near enough to permit of the bombing of Tokyo or any other large cities in Japan. Or, at the worst, it was supposed that aerial attacks would be on so small a scale that they could be adequately dealt with by fighters. This was the view constantly put forward by the Japanese press, which quoted the military authorities as saying that Tokyo was unassailable from the air. The Army came in for a good deal of criticism in consequence when the first raid actually took place.

I happened to be in the Ginza, the main thoroughfare of Tokyo, at the time. The warning was sounded at about five minutes past twelve on Saturday the 18th April, 1942. At first, no one paid very much attention, most of us thinking that the siren was the ordinary midday signal which is sounded in the city every day. This signal had been discontinued on the outbreak of war, but I supposed we had only half-consciously realized it. Almost immediately afterwards, American bombers appeared over the city, flying so low that their distinguishing marks were clearly visible. They appeared to be unopposed, although gunfire now became audible from the distant suburbs. This increased in intensity, particularly from the direction of Yokohama, and continued for several hours; nor was it until about half-past four in the afternoon that the "All Clear" was sounded.[1] There was not the slightest sign of panic. The police halted the traffic, but nobody made any attempt to take shelter; the general sentiment was one of bewildered interest, everybody wondering what was going to happen next. Pedestrians just stood about in groups; and then, as a realization of what was happening gradually dawned upon them, one heard people starting to criticize the army for having misled them.

That night there was a complete blackout, and we were ordered to keep our radios permanently switched on in case special instructions should be issued. Later on, there was an order that in the event of the

[1] I cannot account for the prolonged gunfire. General Doolittle himself told me that none of his aircraft was over the city for more than one hour.

AIR RAID PRECAUTIONS: THE AMERICAN AIR RAID

warning being sounded in the future, radios were to be immediately switched on and not turned off until the raid was over.

The evening papers gave only the bare news that a raid had taken place, but details were given in the late news broadcast. We were told that no damage had been done; and that seven, possibly eight, of the American planes had been brought down. Although it was claimed that no casualties had occurred, there was a notice in the papers about one week later to the effect that the government intended to grant full compensation to all those who had suffered loss or injury in the raid.

Soon after my return to England I had the opportunity of discussing the raid with General James Doolittle, who led it. The General told me that while most of the twenty-five planes which took part in the raid were to some extent holed by anti-aircraft fire, all but two returned safely to their bases. Moreover, none of the men who took part in the raid was wounded. I heard through a neutral Embassy that as soon as it was known that several American aircraft had been downed, the Axis air attachés asked for permission to examine the wreckage. The request, however, was categorically refused.

There was a great deal of speculation as to the base from which the raid was carried out. Several days later the Japanese Navy issued a statement that the American raiders were known to have taken off from two, or possibly three, aircraft-carriers which were part of a force operating in the North Pacific. The official opinion was that the aircraft were launched from a point some 1,400 miles east and slightly north of Yokohama, or half-way between that port and Dutch Harbour.

When I asked General Doolittle if this surmise was correct he gave a smile, then said: " That's quite a question, isn't it? " But the mystery surrounding the operation has now been cleared up by an official statement issued in the United States on the 18th April, 1943, the first anniversary of the raid. The secret base, up till then referred to by President Roosevelt as " Shangri La," was in fact the aircraft-carrier " Hornet," which was subsequently sunk in the battle of Santa Cruz Islands, on the 26th October last year. It had been arranged that the aircraft should take off when about 400 miles from Tokyo, but a meeting with a Japanese naval force led to last-minute changes and an 800-mile flight was made to Japan. This increased distance meant that the aircraft could not reach their scheduled landing-grounds in China. General Doolittle himself baled out over China, and other aeroplanes made forced or crash landings, owing to lack of petrol, in China or in the sea off the China coast. One landed in Russia. The official disclosure added that of the eighty men who took part in the raid, five were interned in Russia, eight were prisoners in Japan, two were missing and one killed. The other sixty-four, many of them after long delays, made their way to various camps of the Chinese army and thence to American territory. Although none of the planes was brought down by enemy action, the possession by the Japanese of certain prisoners is probably due to the fact that one of the aircraft made a forced landing in a part of China which is at present in Japanese occupation. Some of these prisoners, it now appears, have already been executed by the Japanese. It seems unnecessary to comment upon this barbarous disregard of the terms of the Geneva convention.

By piecing together odd scraps of information it gradually became possible to find out what had really happened in Tokyo. It appears that several hundred people who were working in a factory were wounded. The petrol storage tank at Haneda aerodrome, Tokyo's civil airport, was set on fire and continued to burn for several days following the raid. There was considerable damage to the military aerodrome a short distance outside Tokyo, and several streets of houses in the vicinity of Waseda University were demolished. All this was reported to me personally by friends who actually witnessed it. The total damage done was doubtless much greater.

The immense distance the planes had to cover before reaching their objectives greatly increased the risks involved, and it may be wondered whether the raid was worth while, especially as it was, of necessity, not on a very big scale. The actual amount of damage caused was possibly unimportant, but it should be remembered that the Japanese could not be sure that further raids would not follow. The Americans, by proving the practical possibility of raiding Tokyo, probably caused them to keep back a large number of first-line aircraft which would otherwise have been sent to the various theatres of war. And as the Pacific campaign develops, the threat of further raids on Japan will cause the Japanese to keep still larger numbers of aircraft in reserve for the defence of their home country.

At about four o'clock in the morning on the day following the raid there was a further alarm in Tokyo. Lying in bed I heard what sounded like a large force of Japanese planes passing over my house; but nothing happened, and the " All Clear " was sounded about one hour later.

There was yet another alarm at eleven o'clock on Sunday morning. Large numbers of Japanese fighters were visible in the sky, and a certain amount of distant gunfire was to be heard. This time, in accordance with the official instructions, I spent the morning on guard at my front door, the regulation bucket of water and sandbags beside me: but again there were no incidents. The " All Clear " was sounded at about one-thirty, and at two o'clock it was announced by radio that a large enemy force had attempted to approach the capital, but had been driven off before it was able to penetrate even the outer defences. I believe that no attempt was made to raid Tokyo a second time, and that the whole affair was an imposture devised by the authorities to win back the confidence of the people. If so, it had some success, for I noticed that in my own street many of the older people seemed to gain courage on hearing that the raiders had been thwarted in an attempt to reach the city.

It was an odd experience to be bombed by one's own side, but my sentiment at the time was one of satisfaction, for I had been feeling ill at ease. It seemed wrong that, after five months of war, life in Japan should still be so near to normal. I devoutly hoped that this first raid was the prelude to worse ones to come; and although far from wishing to be blown to bits myself, I suffered bitter and increasing disappointment when nothing further happened. By some unaccountable operation of the mind I felt personally responsible for the calm that followed.

I have said that the American aircraft which carried out the raid flew very low over the city. They actually came in, General Doolittle told me, at tree-top level, thus avoiding a great deal of the anti-aircraft fire. I believe that before this raid there was no defence against low-flying aircraft, but shortly afterwards machine-gun posts were visible on many of the buildings in the central part of Tokyo. Barrage balloons also made their first appearance over the city, but I never saw more than six in the air at the same time. One of these was moored in the centre of Hibiya Park. It was surrounded by a double fence of barbed wire and guarded by sentries with rifles and fixed bayonets who warned off anyone who attempted to approach the enclosure.

★ 7 ★

IN ALL THESE MONTHS I HAD NO MEANS OF FINDING OUT WHAT HAD happened to my friends. During the first few days I had visited several of their houses, only to find the police in charge. They refused to give me any information and told me to keep away. I realized, of course, that most of our nationals had been taken into custody, but I could not discover who was in gaol, who in an internment camp. One evening, however, I was astonished to receive a visit from Mrs. Hawley. Knowing that I was her husband's most intimate friend, her first act on being released from prison was to find out what had happened to me. As a Japanese married to an Englishman she was in a delicate situation. But she never even considered her own personal safety, and, although I begged her to be careful, this brave woman continued to visit me and saw that I was kept supplied with food. I can never repay her for this very great self-sacrifice. I now learned of Hawley's whereabouts, and his wife was also able to give me information about other mutual friends, many of whom she had seen at one time or another in the corridors of the prison.

It appeared that all the British and American journalists were in gaol, but that the majority of the teachers, missionaries, and business men had been interned either in Tokyo or Yokohama. I applied to the police for permission to visit the camp, but this was refused. Internees, I discovered, were permitted to receive visitors at infrequent intervals, but the request had to emanate from them. Later, I discovered that, fearing to implicate me, my friends had not asked for me, but a chance encounter with one in the street, who had been allowed out to see his dentist, gave me the opportunity to put the matter right, and I was eventually able to visit one of the internment camps on several occasions. The conditions there were good, and except for the lack of privacy, better than outside. This was certainly the case with regard to food, ample quantities or which were supplied by the government, in addition to which internees' servants were daily permitted to bring to the camp anything they were able to obtain on the open market.

Strange though it may seem, I would myself much have preferred to have been interned. Although no restrictions were placed upon my movements, and I was even permitted after a time to continue my lectures, I suffered from severe mental strain, as I felt sure it was merely a matter of time before I, too, should be arrested. Not that I was suffering from a guilty conscience; but so many people whom I knew to be perfectly harmless had been arrested that there seemed to be no reason why I should be left at liberty. Eventually I reached the stage when I experienced a pang of dread every time my front door bell rang. "At last," I thought, "my moment has come!"

I must here say something of the attitude of my Japanese friends during this period. Not one ceased to visit me, and I even made a few new friends. Some of them went to great personal trouble to keep me supplied with food, and others denied themselves such luxuries as eggs in order that I should not go short. I shall never forget their kindness, nor the risks they took; for in a country like

MY JAPANESE FRIENDS

Japan, with its vicious system of police spying, it requires considerable courage to pay regular visits to an enemy alien in wartime. Some of my friends would attempt to discuss events and did not disguise their dislike of the Japanese military party. I refused, however, to discuss this subject. Cynical though it may seem, I had always to consider the possibility that some among my friends were agents of the police, and that they had perhaps been ordered to keep up their intercourse with me on the chance that I might make some indiscreet remark which would serve as an excuse for my arrest. I did not, of course, really think that any friend of mine would so demean himself; but after even a short time in Japan one becomes suspicious; and I felt that I dare not take the slightest risk. I only hope that since my departure none of my friends has suffered for his constancy; it is a matter which often troubles me as I lie awake at night.

It is the custom in Japan to display the national flag on all occasions of public rejoicing. In peacetime it was no embarrassment to me to conform. After the declaration of war, however, the position was different; I did not feel that the fall of Hong Kong and Singapore, for instance, called for a display of rejoicing on my part, and my undecorated house brought upon me a certain amount of adverse criticism from my neighbours. Eventually, however, a compromise was reached; my cook agreed on my behalf that I should hoist the flag on occasions such as the Emperor's birthday, provided that I should not be expected to celebrate the allied reverses, which at that time were occurring with depressing frequency. As for the pound of sugar and two bottles of beer which everyone was allowed to purchase in order to mark the surrender of Singapore, I must confess that I gratefully accepted them.

It must have been about this time that I was asked to contribute towards the purchase of aeroplanes for the Japanese army. I explained that as a British subject I could hardly be expected to subscribe towards the bombing of my own people, but this was a point of view that did not commend itself to the collector. The fact that I was not interned had given him to think that I must be a traitor to my country, or at least not in sympathy with its war aims, and I was quite unable to convince him that he was wrong. It was only after arranging to give to the Japanese Red Cross the amount of the subscription he demanded for his aeroplanes that I induced him to go away. Little things of this sort were constantly happening; they were tiresome, but they helped me to retain my sense of humour.

But aeroplanes were not the only objects for which subscriptions were demanded: comforts for the troops, war memorials, government war bonds, even liquid refreshments for voluntary A.R.P.

AMUSEMENTS; CHANGES IN EDUCATION

workers were among the things to which I was at one time or another asked to contribute. And there was in addition a compulsory savings scheme, under which every householder was forced to invest a weekly sum according to his income, but what became of the money so collected I was never able to discover. The collector for all these various " charities " was in every case either the head of the local Neighbourhood Association or one of his underlings; and as he was also the man in charge of ration-distribution the greatest tact was called for in dealing with him. What I should have done without my cook I do not know.

The effect of this organized government extortion will, I imagine, result in widespread debt, particularly among the poorer classes, for it should be remembered that the average Japanese lives up to the limit of his income; and during the last year or so the cost of living had risen enormously. In addition to this, the government has " encouraged " firms to pay at least some proportion of their employees' salaries in the form of government bonds. To a man with a family, who probably needs every penny he can earn in order to pay for the bare necessities of life, these bonds are of hardly more use than so much waste paper. On the top of all this, too, the wretched Japanese is urged to marry at the earliest possible moment and to raise as many children as he can, no matter what his financial position may be. It is true that there now exists a scheme by which assistance is granted to young married couples who agree to co-operate with the government in its plan for increasing the size of the Japanese army; but the benefits offered are out of all proportion to the actual expense involved, and none but the ultra-nationalistic look upon the scheme with any satisfaction. It has been said that when Japan entered the war she staked everything she had on success or defeat. Certain it is that she has gambled recklessly with the health of her future population.

★ *8* ★

I HAVE SAID THAT FOR SOME LITTLE TIME AFTER THE OUTBREAK OF WAR there was little outward change in the life of the Japanese people. An accumulation of small changes, however, was taking place, and these gradually made the people conscious of the war. Most of these changes were concerned with amusement.

AMUSEMENTS; CHANGES IN EDUCATION

After the first week, for instance, a ban was placed upon American and English music, and more particularly upon all forms of jazz. This even extended to the withdrawal from the shops of all foreign gramophone records, not excluding German classical music if the conductor of the orchestra concerned happened not to be a citizen of one or other of the Axis countries. This ban fell heavily upon recordings made by Stokowski and Sir Thomas Beecham, but Toscanini and the many famous German conductors who had long since severed their connection with their own country escaped, their political views being apparently unknown to the Japanese police.

Certain difficulties naturally arose in connection with the New Symphony Orchestra in Tokyo, seeing that its conductor, Mr. Joseph Rosenstock, was of partly Jewish origin. The German Embassy had, of course, long wished to see him removed. Failing in this, it had refused to take cognizance of his existence, so that no member of the diplomatic corps was able to attend his concerts. This, then, seemed a suitable opportunity to raise again the question of his removal. Mr. Rosenstock could hardly be dismissed for inefficiency, for everybody realized that during the few years in which he had been in command, the orchestra had improved out of all recognition. The police, however, by distorting the facts of his private life, which was in fact exemplary, were able to bring a false accusation of immoral conduct against him. The charge was so flimsy that no attempt was made to substantiate it. The police, however, made it clear to him that in his own interests he would be well advised to resign.

The orchestra was now renamed the National Symphony Orchestra and it was actually proposed that its members, instead of wearing the usual evening clothes as heretofore, should appear in the dismal and drab National Uniform which the government had been trying unsuccessfully for several years to popularize. The orchestra, however, refused.

A few concerts were held under the leadership of various Japanese conductors, but the results were so unpleasing that after a few weeks Mr. Rosenstock was induced to return, and at a much larger salary, or so rumour had it, than he had been previously receiving. This story, unimportant in itself, provides a good illustration of Japanese mind and method.

The police could not, of course, examine all the gramophone records already in the possession of private individuals, and many of my friends told me that when playing over their Stokowski recordings their pleasure was heightened by the knowledge that they were forbidden.

The ban on jazz music affected particularly the numerous little tea and coffee shops dotted about all over the city. When it was first enforced, the gramophones in these places were silent; but only for a week or so. At first the records were played very softly, but the volume was soon increased for the people began to realize that the police could not distinguish between, say, Duke Ellington, and Mozart. Before I left Japan, jazz had come back into its own, and the gramophones were again going full blast.

There was now another musical problem to be solved. A few English tunes, *Auld Lang Syne* and *Home Sweet Home*, to mention but two, had been familiar to the Japanese for so long that many people did not even know the country of their origin. It was therefore found necessary to publish an official list of all the " enemy " songs which were considered innocuous. The list was prefaced with a note to the effect that the songs in question had by this time become so completely transformed and adapted to Japanese ideas that no harm could come from them, provided that they were not sung with the English words.

In order to ensure that the people should be properly regardful of the importance of discrimination, every broadcast of Western music was prefaced and closed with a few words announcing the nationality of the composer. Although the nine symphonies of Beethoven are probably as well known and appreciated in Japan as they are in England, every performance now ended with the statement: " You have been listening to a symphony by Mr. Beethoven, the well-known German composer."

As for films, all the American and English ones were immediately withdrawn from circulation, their place being taken by French and German films. Among the latter were many of the excellent pre-Hitler *Ufa* productions which (their directors being Jewish) are no longer shown in Germany itself. To me personally it was a great joy to see once again the early films made by René Clair, but by the time I left Japan most of these old films, which were not very numerous, were being shown for the third or fourth time. There were, of course, plenty of Japanese films, but the urban audiences, having been brought up on foreign films, did not take to them very kindly. They were more popular, I believe, with less sophisticated people in the country districts.

The theatre, too, received the attentions of the police. There were in Tokyo a number of small theatres which specialized in the production of Western plays in the Japanese language. And as English has always been the most widely known of foreign tongues, most of the plays produced were translations from English. Even in peacetime these theatres had a certain amount of trouble with

AMUSEMENTS; CHANGES IN EDUCATION

the police. It is on record that on at least one occasion a licence to perform *Hamlet* was refused on the grounds that it depicted royalty in an unfavourable light and might, therefore, reflect discredit upon the Japanese royal family. These theatrical companies were not actually disbanded, but conditions were now made so difficult for them that the players were forced to appear in plays of purely Japanese origin.

The *Kabuki* theatre, presenting, as it does, traditional Japanese drama, suffered less change. The police were content with the elimination of all plays of a purely comic character and the complete suppression of those in which amorous adventures were represented. In normal times the *Kabuki* programmes include excerpts from several different plays, so arranged as to appeal to all types of audience. Thus, they would usually start with an extract from some play dealing with quiet domestic life in the country. This would be followed by the chief items of the evening, generally a couple of blood-and-thunder historical dramas; then would come a somewhat boisterous and erotic comedy; and the evening would be rounded off with the Japanese equivalent of a ballet.

The menu now was one of unrelieved blood and thunder. Moreover, most of the plays were so edited as to be little more than exhortations to patriotism. The virtue of dying for one's betters, that is to say for one's country, was instilled to the exclusion of any other theme. All the ordinary aims, aspirations, and loves of human beings were excluded.

All this contributes to the great change which is coming over Japanese education. Its effects are not yet fully apparent in the upper-grade schools and universities, but children are growing up with minds so warped that their re-education, after the defeat of Japan, is likely to present as great a problem as is that of the youth of Hitler's Germany.

In the primary and middle schools throughout the whole country only books recommended by the Department of Education may now be used. In spite of the acute paper shortage, most of these textbooks have been re-written: world history, economics, indeed every subject is now presented to the growing child from an exaggeratedly nationalistic point of view. The white races are everywhere represented as oppressors whose decadence is ushering in their destruction. At the same time, of course, much is made of Japan's contributions to the thought, culture, and progress of the world. This has had extraordinary repercussions on some of the more chauvinistic adults. In the months following the outbreak of war, I saw in the press articles claiming that the aeroplane was a

Japanese invention, and that the Japanese were responsible for most of the major discoveries of modern science. Perhaps the most extraordinary of all was an article purporting to prove that Christ had been born somewhere in the north of Japan. It is easy to laugh at these absurd claims which, of course, are not believed by the intelligent and educated. The fact remains, however, that a large proportion of the population accepts, as indeed it does in most countries, what it reads in the press as true. And the Japanese, perhaps more than most people, are only too ready to believe anything that redounds to their own credit.[1]

The most dangerous changes have taken place in what could be roughly described as moral training. The growing child is now taught, almost from infancy, that its primary duty is not to its parents but to the state, to which it belongs, to be done with as the state desires.[2] It is taught to worship the armed forces, and told that the greatest honour is to die in battle. I always found it a frightening and pathetic sight to see little children, many of them so young that they could barely walk, saluting the soldiers with which the streets are everywhere now crowded.

The real change in mentality will not be fully apparent until the children at present under sixteen complete their education. When that happens there will be in Japan an adult population that believes solidly in its country's divine mission. At present it is not so. The present generation of university students, whose preliminary education was completed in comparatively enlightened times, possess for the most part a liberal outlook. But even they have not escaped the net of the chauvinistic reformer. The courses in all High Schools throughout the country were shortened from three years to two. The three-year syllabus remained unchanged, but the loss of the final year was balanced by the complete abolition of all vacations. I have pointed out elsewhere that the competition to enter these High Schools is so great that already a high proportion of the successful

---

[1] Following upon the reorganization of Christian worship throughout Greater East Asia, the Japanese have embarked upon a campaign to re-write the bible. The following extract is taken from a recent (April 1943) broadcast entitled *Church News Commentary*: " It is a well known fact that the history of different versions of the Holy Scriptures all too often was the history of the progress of Christianity. We have the great pleasure to report that a new translation of the Old Testament is well under way. . . . This new translation of the Bible by Japanese scholars is most timely."

[2] Lecturing the Burmans on the proper treatment of children, a Japanese commentator, broadcasting from Rangoon in April 1943, ended his talk with the following words: " In the final issue, children (i.e. Burman children) belong to the Emperor." So much for Burman independence!

AMUSEMENTS; CHANGES IN EDUCATION

entrants break down before graduating. Now that the students are required to go through their two year course without more than a break of an odd day or so, it is reasonable to suppose that breakdowns will considerably increase. This fact was indeed realized by most of the more responsible teachers, and shortly before I left the country a deputation made a protest to the Minister of Education. He was, I believe, sympathetic, but unable to do anything, since the army, which now controls the whole of Japanese life, was unwilling to make any concession that would impede the rapid flow of recruits.[1]

In the universities the same system was adopted, and an additional regulation was introduced by which any students who had not graduated on reaching the age of twenty-five immediately became liable for military service. It should be noted that this affected many more students than would be the case in a European university, since, on account of the difficulties of the Japanese language itself and of the absolute necessity of acquiring a good knowledge of at least one foreign language, the average age of graduation is much higher in Japan than in any other country.

Apart from all this, however, the amount of military training in all schools and universities has been considerably increased. Military training has always been compulsory in Japanese schools, but in the best of them it was formerly not allowed to interfere unduly with the more serious business of education. Army officers, two or three of which are now attached to every male educational institution throughout the country, are in theory subject to the orders of the head of the school concerned. In actual practice, however, very few head masters now dare oppose them, as a result of which they are able to exert considerable influence on education. This they do by ordering extra military parades during such hours as the students would otherwise be studying what the military officers doubtless consider useless subjects, philosophy, literature, indeed, anything which has no direct military value. During my last few months I went many times to the classroom, only to find it empty because my students had been taken away for extra military training.

These new regulations have been applied not only to students of the arts, but, with reckless disregard for the country's future needs, even to the faculties of science, engineering, and medicine.

In the European and American press attention has frequently been drawn to the fact that Japan is, and always has been, an extremely militarily-minded nation. In my experience, however, there is

[1] Recent reports indicate that education has been again curtailed and the hours devoted to military training still further increased. In April 1943 the Prime Minister, General Tojo, became concurrently Minister for Education.

among the present generation of university students fairly widespread dislike of the army, and I have little doubt that even to-day, if it were left to individual choice, only a comparatively small number of them would enlist. Many of the students in my own classes seized every opportunity to absent themselves from military training, and there was always a good deal of passive resistance to the officers in charge of military instruction. This may seem strange in a nation so long accustomed to discipline as the Japanese. In Japanese schools and universities, however, the students have always had a say (none the less weighty for not being officially recognized) in the selection of their teachers. An unpopular or inefficient lecturer will find his classroom more or less empty. Nothing is ever said by the students or by the school authorities, but the teacher concerned will presently find himself relieved of his duties. To-day, the students cannot absent themselves from military training without some very good excuse. They have, however, found methods of showing their dislike of military training in excess.

It is my impression that among the better type of university graduates there is considerable unwillingness to accept a commission in the army. In former times there was, of course, no question of giving conscripts commissioned rank, the officer cadre being formed entirely of graduates from the Military Academy who had made the army their chosen profession. Since the war, however, all university graduates, after a certain period in the ranks, have been forced to sit for the examination to commissioned rank. One or two of those personally known to me defeated this regulation by handing in completely blank papers at the end of the examination, but I know of at least one case where a candidate who did this was informed several days later that he had successfully passed the test.

It is important not to overrate this dislike of military service. It applies only to what is, after all, a very small (though important) section of the community, and I have only drawn attention to it here in order to suggest that the Japanese are not quite so wholeheartedly behind their military leaders as is commonly supposed. It should not be assumed that these unwilling conscripts make bad soldiers. I shall have something to say about this in a chapter dealing with actual conditions in the Japanese army.

PERSONAL STORY

★ 9 ★

AFTER THE 8TH DECEMBER I HAD VERY LITTLE TO DO. I HAVE ALREADY explained that as soon as things began to settle down I was permitted to continue with my lectures, but these occupied only a few hours every week. The Foreign Office continued to pay my salary but relieved me of all duties, so I had a great deal of time on my hands. It might have been an excellent opportunity to set down one's ideas on paper, or at least to keep a diary. This, however, was impossible. It is not advisable, while actually in the country, to commit one's thoughts on Japan to paper, unless they happen to be entirely flattering; even in normal times the Japanese police surreptitiously make periodical examinations of the contents of all foreigners' houses. And, when the time came to leave, it was forbidden to take any letters, manuscripts, or even a book, out of the country, irrespective of the contents.

I used at first to spend many hours a day listening to records on my gramophone and reading. During these months I read the whole of Meredith, most of Henry James, and all the Brontë novels. But I obtained my greatest pleasure from the discovery of Richardson. *Pamela* and *Clarissa* helped me through many difficult hours; I did not even boggle at Grandison's interminable conversations in the Cedar Parlour. *Middlemarch*, too, was a great solace, but re-reading *The Private Papers of Henry Ryecroft* produced only a feeling of almost unbearable nostalgia. Many other books I read, including much of Carlyle (which I found intolerable), but it is only those I have mentioned that really helped me at the time. After a while I ceased to play the gramophone. I am affected more by music than by any other form of art, and during these months I reached a stage when the emotional effect of hearing great music was so overpowering that I could no longer bear it.

Nearly every afternoon I used to go to the Imperial Hotel, which still retained its vogue in spite of the fact that the food it now provided was about the worst in Tokyo. For one thing there was a great influx of newly-rich Japanese, of the type who do not know good food from bad, at any rate so far as foreign dishes are concerned. And then, just because a large proportion of the hotel shares were owned by members of the Imperial family, the management felt it a duty to make the menus even more austere than they need be. I cannot imagine why the hotel still retained its popularity with foreigners, unless it was because it was one of the very few places in Tokyo where the chairs approximated to a European standard of comfort.

At teatime the place was usually crowded with Nazis, and it used to give me a peculiar pleasure to sit there and be glared at. For they knew, of course, exactly who I was, and it doubtless infuriated them to see me still at large. Incidentally, although Tokyo contained a considerable Italian colony, I never once saw Italians mixing with Germans, except on public platforms, where they had of necessity to make a show of friendliness.

I was lucky in having a few anti-Nazi friends of German birth, but as time went on it became increasingly difficult to meet them. Some of them, being Jewish, had already lost their citizenship and there was, therefore, no reason why they should not associate with me. Among them was one whose wife was Japanese. He had married her many years before, but she was still without a word of German. Being an "honorary Aryan," however, she now found herself in the strange situation of being a German citizen, while her husband, who had been born and bred in Austria, was without any nationality.

But my two most intimate friends were not Jewish; they were anti-Nazi by conviction. The German Embassy made constant efforts to bring them into the fold, but in spite of threats to retaliate against their relatives in Germany, they remained faithful to their convictions. Shortly before I left, both of them were officially expatriated, and under the orders of the German Embassy denied employment in any German company. Both have high technical qualifications and will doubtless obtain employment with some Japanese firm, for the Embassy had been unsuccessful in its efforts to persuade the Japanese government to prohibit the employment of the German citizens of whom it disapproved. I ought perhaps to make it clear that of the very large numbers of Germans now in Tokyo, by no means all are Nazis, many of them having come to Japan in order to escape persecution in their own country.

As for the relations between the Germans and the Japanese, the attitude of the ordinary people towards their German allies is well illustrated by an incident that occurred shortly before I left Tokyo. It was a pouring wet night and I was in the street looking for a taxi to take me home. I eventually found one, but the driver eyed me askance as a foreigner. After a little talk, however, he seemed more friendly, but as I was about to open the door he demurred again. "Are you a German?" he asked. "No; certainly not," I replied.

"An Italian, then, perhaps?" For a moment I considered passing myself off as an Italian in order to get a lift, and he, noticing my hesitation, enquired bluntly what my nationality was. "As a matter of fact," I said, "I'm English," to which he replied with a cheerful grin, "Oh; all right, hop in!"

It is not difficult to account for the dislike in which the Germans are held. Most of them are extremely arrogant and make no attempt to disguise their contempt for the Japanese. Moreover, few educated Japanese are ignorant of Hitler's published views on the peoples of Asia.

In official, but non-military, circles, it is the same story. Of recent years German advisers have been admitted into several government departments, and this has led to constant friction. The Nazi cannot advise; he can only dictate. And while the Japanese have always been willing to accept guidance from their various foreign advisers, dictation they will accept from nobody. At one time a couple of Germans were attached to the Tokyo Central Post Office. They had been planted there by the Embassy ostensibly for the purpose of examining the correspondence of German residents. It was not long, however, before they demanded access to the correspondence of all foreigners, and when this was refused they became so offensive that the Japanese officials insisted on their withdrawal. Then there was the case of a certain Colonel Meissinger, a notorious member of the Gestapo, who had been sent to Japan in order to give the police the benefit of his experience. Standing in the hall of the Imperial Hotel, this gentleman would boast loudly of the number of people he had shot with his own hand. He took it as part of his present mission to bully the Japanese police into arresting not only anti-Nazi Germans, but all foreigners who were regarded unfavourably by the German Embassy.

In military circles the position is different. There is no doubt that the professional Japanese Army officer has a high regard for the Germans, or perhaps it would be more correct to say that he has a great respect for the German Army. After all, the Japanese army has been organized and trained on German lines, and under the supervision of German experts. This does not necessarily mean that Japan's strategical plans have been worked out in close conjunction with Germany's. The Japanese were quick to note that the commencement of Hitler's retirement in Russia coincided with the day they themselves entered the war, and it is doubtful whether they have ever had any illusion about getting material assistance from Germany, no matter how things might turn out. There must obviously be a certain amount of co-operation between the General

Staffs of the two countries, but the Japanese are realists and are in this war for their own ends alone.

The Japanese Navy is even less " pro-German," and this is natural seeing that the British Navy served it as a model, and that at one time officers of that Navy were attached to it as instructors.

A few people who have returned from the Far East during the last year or two have described the Japanese as pro-British. This, in my opinion, is a completely false view of the situation. It would, however, be true to say that in liberal and intellectual circles there are many people who are not anti-British, by which I mean to imply that they do not entertain any feeling of hatred towards us. The Japanese of the best type have always held British culture and British methods in high regard; but this does not imply that they want us to win the war. In the secrecy of their own hearts not a few hope for a German defeat, to be followed, in the Eastern theatre of war, by a compromise peace. But this is the point of view of a very small minority; a minority which at the present time has absolutely no power. There should be no doubt about that. When assessing the feeling of the Japanese towards us, one must bear in mind that they have a great capacity for dissociating their private from their national feelings. In fact, one of the first acts of the government after the outbreak of war was to make the public pronouncement that although Japan was now at war with Britain this should not be allowed to interfere with individual friendships. Characteristically, however, the government lost no time in imprisoning or interning nearly all British subjects. Indeed, I was the only one to be given complete freedom. But even in the months immediately preceding the outbreak of war, during which time we were certainly not in favour, there was no real anti-British feeling. It is true that numerous meetings of protest were held, and on several occasions there were demonstrations outside the British Embassy. But these all took place at the instigation of various reactionary societies, in some cases with the active support of the army. Never at any time did they receive the support of the people; there was nothing spontaneous about them.

★ 10 ★

WHEN A RECRUIT JOINS THE JAPANESE ARMY THE FIRST THING HE IS taught is that he must look upon dying as a duty. This is impressed upon him constantly, not only in verbal exhortations, but by posters which are stuck up in every barrack room.

In the past few years quite a number of books have been written by Japanese soldiers describing their experiences in the China campaign. The authors, for the most part, are cripples or men who have been otherwise incapacitated, but in spite of this they always open their books with a humble apology for being alive. Nor is this an empty formula; there is no doubt that the Japanese soldier who returns to enjoy civilian life really does feel that he has failed in his duty to the country. This feeling also accounts for the shame felt by the Japanese who are taken prisoner. Some foreign observers have derided this state of mind, but, in my opinion, wrongly, for in the individual soldier's willingness to die lies the strength of the Japanese army. The sentiment has often been described as fanaticism; but it equally deserves the name of bravery. We should be unwise to decry it or to refuse to recognize wherein the strength of our enemies lies. I have not the slightest doubt that the United Nations will, in their own good time, defeat the Japanese; but they will do so all the quicker if they realize the toughness of the enemy that opposes them.

One of the reasons why we have underrated the military efficiency of the Japanese is that they themselves have always made elaborate arrangements that we should. They are past-masters in trickery, and they have on occasion gone to what might be considered absurd lengths to deceive foreign observers into drawing wrong conclusions.

I remember a dinner-party at the British Embassy at which a young American officer described his impressions of the Japanese army, to which he had been attached for several months past. He had come back filled with contempt for the seeming inefficiency of every branch of the service. Communications were always going wrong; the signalling equipment was years out of date; and in particular the Japanese machine guns had an effective range markedly inferior to that of the guns used by his own army, and so on. We all felt pleased and reassured, for I don't think it occurred to anyone at the time that what the young man had actually seen was nothing more nor less than an elaborately staged piece of imposture.

Then, too, there was an exhibition in Tokyo at which were displayed models of the various types of military aircraft produced by the different countries of the world. Most of the great nations contributed, sending, if not their latest models, some of fairly recent design. As for the Japanese exhibits, a friend of mine who was imprisoned after the war was told with pride by the Japanese police that prior to the exhibition a meeting had been held to decide, not, as might be supposed, what were the latest models that might with safety be shown, but what were the most obsolete designs that could be exhibited without arousing suspicion.

A military parade is held in Tokyo on the first of January every year, in the course of which some thousand aeroplanes fly in formation over the city. Before the war it was noticeable that all the aircraft taking part in this manoeuvre were, compared with those used by other armies, obsolescent. On New Year's Day of 1942, however, up-to-date bombers and fighters appeared in the parade for the first time; by then, of course, there was no longer any object in trying to deceive foreign observers.

For a great many years the Japanese have been taking elaborate precautions to conceal their real military training. Certain areas of the country have been designated as defended zones or special military areas, and no unauthorized Japanese, let alone a foreigner, would dare to venture anywhere near them. The Japanese went to extraordinary lengths to deceive the outside world, and with some success apparently, for there is no doubt that everybody greatly underestimated their efficiency.

A great deal of training is now carried on in public parks and other open spaces in Tokyo. Even the streets in crowded parts of the city are used at any time of the day or night for practising streetfighting. I frequently found myself held up for fifteen or twenty minutes in the Tokyo equivalent of Whitehall while some manoeuvre was in progress.

All movements are carried out in double time, even when it is a question of changing the position of a heavy machine-gun from one place to another.

Route marches of thirty to forty miles seem to be part of the training; and often they are ended with a half-mile double. I have been told that the Japanese soldier never falls out during a march, and certainly I myself have seen men returning from a long march obviously on the verge of collapse. Some were being dragged along by their comrades with ropes.

THE JAPANESE ARMY

Judged by European standards, discipline is harsh. An open space outside one of the schools where I taught was used as a practice ground for artillery units, and on several occasions I saw recruits knocked unconscious by non-commissioned officers. This was done in the presence of higher ranks, so I can only suppose that such behaviour was customary.

The Japanese idea of discipline is based on fear; the soldier is taught not to think but only to obey. This applies also to the corps of officers. Some of my friends who have had the opportunity to observe the army at close quarters have told me that Japanese regimental officers are exceedingly efficient so long as they are not called upon to deal with a situation for which no provision has been made in their official text-books. In novel situations they are apparently apt to lose their heads. It would seem that this weakness is known to the higher command, for there is little doubt that the Japanese army does not, as a rule, undertake any offensive operation before having done the most elaborate rehearsing, during the course of which the smallest details are practised over and over again; nothing is left to chance.

The reader will perhaps find this difficult to believe in view of the great success obtained by the Japanese troops in their campaigns in Malaya and Burma. These operations were often carried out in what had hitherto been thought of as impenetrable jungle, and the nature of the fighting was such as called for a high degree of individual initiative in junior officers. It should be remembered, however, that before they embarked upon these campaigns the units of the Japanese army which took part in them received specialized training in the jungles of French Indo-China for one whole year. This was made possible by the co-operation of the Vichy government.

Side by side with this harsh discipline there runs an odd strain of democratic feeling, which owes its existence to the fact that the professional officers of the Japanese army are not normally drawn from the higher social levels of society. I have frequently seen private soldiers occupying seats in buses and underground trains with generals (as numerous in Tokyo as nowadays in London) straphanging beside them. The private would invariably stand up and salute the officer when he entered the train, but having done this would then resume his seat. Incidentally, in the Japanese army all soldiers are required to salute anyone who is their senior, including, of course, private soldiers of a grade superior to their own. The effect of this in a crowded place is that they seem never to cease saluting.

I should say that the training in general was much more rigorous than in any European army. My house in Tokyo was not far from one of the big military rifle-ranges, and even in peacetime I used frequently to hear shooting between two and three o'clock in the morning, and that even in winter with the rain coming down.

On first joining the service, recruits are treated with particular strictness. For the first few weeks they are not even allowed to write letters, and during their first six months of training they are confined to barracks. After this they are given one free day a month, usually a Sunday. All letters written from barracks are strictly censored, as, of course, is all incoming correspondence.

Conscripts in Japan are divided into three classes. The first includes all those whose physique is sufficiently good to permit of their immediate enlistment upon reaching the age limit. The necessary medical examination takes place at about the age of nineteen, in many cases while the prospective recruit is still at school.

In the second category are those of slightly inferior physique. Up to the time I left Japan, these lads were not being called up until about one year after medical examination. This class is looked upon as the first reserve of the army, and in normal times those placed in it are not called upon to serve. They receive no training and merely remain as potential reserves until they pass the age limit. Before the war, very few conscripts were taken from the towns, the army being able to meet all its normal requirements by recruitment from the country districts.

The third class consists of all those who fail to pass the medical examination. Men in this category are normally exempt from all military obligations, but a few whom I knew personally were called up for further examination last year and taken into the service. Some of them had reached the age of thirty and were, I should say, quite unfit for a life of active service.

Defective sight is not considered any bar to service, even in the navy. I have often seen sailors wearing spectacles, the very thick lenses of which showed them to be suffering from pronounced myopia. It is only comparatively recently that the British army has accepted recruits whose vision needs correction. Behind this there lies, I believe, a regard for appearances, spectacles being held to give the face a pacific rather than a military aspect. A scientific friend of mine tells me, however, that these short-sighted persons are not congenitally deficient in the warlike spirit.

But long before the war Japanese prowess in all forms of sport and athletics (some of their best performers are extremely short-sighted) should have convinced us that the Anglo-Saxon dislike of spectacled soldiers was based merely on the ancient prejudices of the " spit and polish " school.

The physical examination of recruits is very thorough. Great care is taken to ensure that the prospective soldier is not suffering from incipient tuberculosis, the lungs of every candidate being X-rayed. In view of the now widespread incidence of tuberculosis in the army as well as among civilians, I cannot help feeling that a large number of sufferers from this disease escape detection. Or, possibly, the X-ray examination has been retained as a mere matter of form, little attention being paid to its results, in view of the urgent needs of the services.

Prospective recruits are examined at the military headquarters nearest their place of birth, and as the population of the large cities always contains very large numbers of young men whose real homes are in the country, and whose physique has inevitably deteriorated as a result of unhealthy city life, this rule has some importance. Large numbers of potential recruits would appear to be lost to the service, for such men, if examined with a view to enlistment in the urban regiments, in which the physical standard is lower, would in most cases pass the test. Among the many hundreds of students personally known to me it often happened that many obviously weak candidates were accepted, whereas others, equally obviously much more physically fit, were rejected because they were examined with a view to enlistment in country regiments. Incidentally, I was often told that the Higher Command does not have a high opinion of regiments recruited in the cities, Tokyo itself having the worst reputation in this respect. The best regiments are said to come from the southern island of Kyushu, where life is healthy and the old feudal military tradition is more potent than anywhere else. Kyushu has always provided the Japanese army with a great many of its most successful generals and high naval officers. In the past it was famous for being the birthplace of the majority of Japan's most progressive statesmen; to-day the position is reversed, for Kyushu now produces a majority of the most reactionary elements in the country.

Before leaving the subject of the army, I must say something about the garrison of Manchuria. This is usually referred to as the Kwantung army, and it is well known to be the flower of the armed forces of Japan, both officers and men having been carefully selected over a long period of years. The Japanese at least have never underrated the military might of Soviet Russia. The Kwantung army is kept up to strength by reinforcements who have particularly distinguished themselves in the various theatres of war in which the Japanese army is now operating.

The Kwantung army first came into prominence in 1931, when it set about annexing Manchuria without troubling to obtain the sanction of the home government. It is from this date that the army, having successfully taken the bit between its teeth, started to acquire its now overwhelming control over politics. The Kwantung army has always been politically-minded and undoubtedly has great influence in the selection of the Minister for War. Curiously enough, it is at least doubtful whether the supreme command itself has much political power, the real guiding force being the semi-secret political societies composed of comparatively junior officers. Concerning their activities very little is known, even to the Japanese people themselves.

It is interesting to speculate whether in certain eventualities the Kwantung army would be loyal to the Emperor, as the head of the government, or to its own commander. It is in some respects similar to the German *Waffen SS.*, which has pledged allegiance to Mr. Hitler as an individual, not as the head of the state. To what extent the Kwantung garrison is an army within the army it is not possible to state, but one can conceive that in a situation such that the Japanese government was forced to acknowledge defeat, the Kwantung army might yet hold out, refusing to accept their government's decision.

Many people have asked me what it is that makes the Japanese army so strong. Behind all more direct answers lies the basic fact that the Japanese are not afraid of death, and hold that there is no greater honour than to die in battle. This makes it possible for the General Staff to risk what in other countries would be looked upon as appallingly heavy casualties. Even if the Japanese people were to discover that these were often unnecessarily high, there would be no public outcry. In point of fact the people are kept in ignorance, the figures of casualties never being made public. There must come a time, of course, when a shortage of manpower begins to be felt; but that time is not yet.

Another question I am often asked is, why have the Japanese had no real success against China, which lacks all modern equipment? Well, I think there is no doubt that the Japanese General Staff originally expected to finish the China war in a matter of months. It is now known that in the early stages of the campaign the Japanese did not employ either their best troops or their most modern weapons and equipment. When they discovered what they were up against they changed their plans; and for the last three years they have been using the China battle front largely as a training ground on which to prepare for the present struggle—a struggle which was undoubtedly envisaged by Japan's military leaders long ago. What they failed to realize, however, was the degree to which the China war was to unify, arouse, and inspire the Chinese people. If they might have defeated China five years ago by putting forward their whole strength, the position has now been completely altered by the heroic stubbornness of the Chinese people with which they have been opposed.

And then, why did our own defences in the Far East fall almost like a pack of cards? In the first place it should be noted that the Japanese troops considerably outnumbered our own. Moreover, they possessed from the start great superiority in the air. Not only did they have many more aircraft, but our own were not of the latest design. These facts alone, however, are insufficient to account for our disastrous defeats. No useful purpose would now be served by concealing the true state of affairs. The fact is that our armies in the Far East were untrained for the particular type of operation they found themselves called upon to undertake. It had, moreover, been assumed that certain regions were impassable by modern armies, but the Japanese forces had received intensive training (in the jungles of Indo-China) with a view to operating in these very districts. More than this, however, our defeat was due to ignorance of the efficiency of the Japanese army and its methods. The Japanese, on the other hand, were extremely well informed of every detail of our defences. It will be long before the whole unpleasant truth can be told, but I have, I think, indicated the main reasons for our defeat. We are beginning to appreciate the strength of the Japanese, and it can at least be said that we were fortunate in early discovering the reasons for our lack of success in the Pacific theatre.

What is the ultimate war aim of the Japanese army? They themselves describe it as the establishment of what is called the " Greater East Asia Co-Prosperity Sphere." It is difficult to find out exactly what this high-sounding phrase really means. Many of my Japanese friends would say quite frankly that they did not know; but a Foreign Office acquaintance of mine, who was something of a cynic, once told me that it could be roughly interpreted, where the Far East is concerned, as a continuation of the British Empire, but with a change of rulers! My own opinion is that the ultimate aim of the army is quite definitely world conquest. This may seem fantastic, but at the time I left Japan people were saying quite openly that if the Allies lost the European war, which at that time seemed not impossible, Germany would be Japan's next objective. In fact, I once heard it said quite seriously that the Japanese army put the nations of the world into three classes; enemies, neutral enemies, and friendly enemies, Japan's Axis partners making up the last class.

Of one thing, at any rate, I am quite certain in my own mind: there is not the remotest chance of the Japanese army cracking. It is an absolutely first-rate fighting machine, and we should be fools to underestimate it. It will go on fighting until the bitter end. Not for one moment do I doubt that we can eventually destroy it, but for that the first pre-requisite is a proper realization of the toughness of the job.

★ 11 ★

DURING ALL THESE MONTHS IT WAS DIFFICULT TO FIND OUT WHAT WAS really happening in Europe. At first, the Japanese did not actually suppress any of the major items of news, but the papers printed them in such a way that their significance could only be properly understood by one skilled at reading between the lines. In course of time, however, one came to measure Allied successes almost entirely by the lack of news; if there was no mention of Libya for weeks at a time one guessed that things were going well there. But when it looked as though the Germans might actually capture Alexandria the news was copious and appeared in headlines on the front page.

Our main source of information was the radio. The short-wave sets in the possession of the Allied embassies were, of course, confiscated upon the outbreak of war, but there were still some in operation in the various neutral embassies, and it was from these that we obtained bits of genuine information from time to time. I used to get them from an anti-Nazi German friend who gleaned them from one or other of the South American legations. It not frequently happened that by the time the news reached me it had undergone considerable changes. In those days one clutched at any straw, and it was natural to try and improve upon the news before passing it on to anyone else. Incidentally, although neutral embassies were permitted to retain their short-wave receivers, they were required by the Japanese government to give an undertaking not to disclose the news they heard, and warned particularly that on no pretext whatever should they listen to the foreign-language broadcasts radiated from Japan to the outside world!

I have forgotten the exact date, but I think it was some time in April 1942, that I was summoned to the Foreign Office. When I went there I was introduced to the chief of the foreign section of the Japan Broadcasting Corporation, for which I had done a certain amount of work before the war. He was extremely affable and talked on general matters for the first ten minutes; then he became less impersonal. He supposed that I must be finding it difficult to make both ends meet, and thought it might be possible to give me some employment as a broadcaster; how did I feel about it? I felt very strongly about it, and I'm afraid I lost my temper. "It seems to me," I said, "that you are asking me to become Japan's 'Lord Haw-Haw,' or have I misunderstood the position?" My questioner was at first nonplussed, for in Japan it is not etiquette to come straight to the point. After hedging a little he was obliged to confess that this was in fact the idea, and he hoped that I would receive the suggestion favourably. I told him that I realized what the consequences of refusing his offer were likely to be, and that I accepted them. In view of the exceptional treatment afforded me I had remained, I said, strictly neutral, although there was, of course, never any doubt where my sympathies lay. And while perfectly appreciating the circumstances in which I, an enemy alien, was placed, in no circumstances would I demean myself by broadcasting anti-British propaganda.

Having got this off my chest I stalked out of the room, fully expecting to be arrested, or at any rate interned the following day. To my surprise, however, nothing further happened until about three weeks later, when I received a letter from the Broadcasting Corporation saying that if I would kindly submit full particulars of my past career they would be glad to consider me for employment. And there the matter ended. Actually, the outcome of this rather trivial incident is not so surprising as at first it seems. Loyalty to one's country is something that every Japanese understands, and had I accepted their offer I think they would have despised me. By not taking any action against me when I refused, they admitted that my conduct was what they would have expected from one of their own people. But the letter had to be sent me; it was a "face-saving" method of neatly closing the incident.

★ *12* ★

AT ABOUT THIS TIME THERE WERE FREQUENT RUMOURS OF EVACUATION. At one time it was only the British and American diplomats who would be allowed to leave; at another we heard that ordinary civilians above the age of forty would be included. No one seemed really to know, and even the Foreign Office was doubtful. I had, of course, registered my name at the Swiss Legation, Switzerland being the protecting power, and expressed my wish to be repatriated; but no one was able to tell me whether, when the time came, I should be allowed to go. Towards the end of May, it seemed pretty certain that the Americans were soon to leave; in fact one of my friends had actually seen a ship in Yokohama harbour being painted with the special marks denoting neutrality. I was not, of course, able to communicate my wishes to anyone in the British Consulate or Embassy.

And then one day I happened to meet one of Paul Rusch's students in a bus. He told me that Paul, who was interned, was being allowed to go back to his house for a few hours the next day in order to settle his affairs prior to sailing for America. I was up at dawn, too excited to sleep very late, and as soon as I decently could I set off for Paul's house, which was at the other end of the city. I could have burst into tears when I saw him; it was like going home after one's first term at school; there was everything and yet nothing for us to say to one another. At last I was able to get news of all my British and American friends, Wills and Phyllis Argall were both in prison, so were Richard Tenelly and several others, but it appeared that all of them were likely to be transferred to an internment camp a few days before sailing. It was not yet known when this would be, and as things turned out, another month passed before they sailed. It was in the course of this talk that I was able to arrange with Paul that he should get me permission to visit the internment camp. At this time there was no question of any repatriation for Englishmen, the official announcement being that the first evacuation was being confined entirely to citizens of the United States. I had heard a rumour to the effect that negotiations between the British and Japanese governments had completely broken down, as a result of which we were likely to be left in Japan until the end of the war. This was certainly a disappointment; but anyhow it was gratifying to know that one's American friends were likely soon to receive their freedom.

About the middle of June, it seemed that the Americans were really to be off at last. They had been given instructions about their baggage and permission to receive a final visit from their friends. The police telephoned to say that I could go out to the internment camp to bid Paul good-bye. It was with mixed feelings that I set off on a Sunday morning. Wills and Tenelly had just arrived from gaol, both looking surprisingly fit in view of what they had been through during the previous eight months. I had no chance of talking much with them as my permit only allowed me to visit Paul; but the officer on duty was lenient, and while I was exchanging a few words with him, Paul slipped away and told Wills to come down into the room as though by accident. I was able to exchange only a few sentences, but it was a relief to learn that Phyllis Argall had also been released. He had not had a chance to speak with her since the day of their arrest, but he knew that she had now been taken back to her own flat, and he urged me to try and see her.

The next day I telephoned to Phyllis with success, although there was a police officer in charge of her. Either because he was an exceptionally humane specimen of his kind, or because he had received no instructions to the contrary, he raised no objections to my visiting Phyllis. So I lost no time in going to her flat. She told me she was just starting out for the office of *Japan News Week* when she was arrested. My article on Virginia Woolf, which I had handed over to her at Paul's house the night before, was in her handbag and now reposes in the archives of the Japanese police. During the course of her examination she was shown photostatic copies of every letter she had written and received over a period of several years, further evidence, if any is needed, of the thoroughness of the Japanese. No case was proved against either Wills or Phyllis Argall, but both were given suspended sentences of, as far as I can remember, eighteen months. The same treatment was in fact meted out to all the arrested journalists: every one of them was given a sentence, varying apparently with the time he had been in the country, but in no case was anyone required to serve his sentence.

The Americans had been told to let their friends know that they would be allowed to exchange parting words with them at the station before they boarded the special train to Yokohama. I spread the news about as far as I could, and on the morning of departure there must have been at least a couple of hundred Japanese waiting at the station to say good-bye. When I got there at about ten o'clock in the morning, the yard was already picketed by police, and there was a double line of them guarding the approach to the special waiting-room. We supposed that in due course we should be allowed in, but, to my surprise, after about half an hour the police started taking the names of all the Japanese who were present; one or two were even taken away for examination. I stayed on, as, although the police had asked me why I was waiting they had not ordered me away, and I thought there was little likelihood of my being arrested. But I was given no opportunity of saying good-bye to any of my friends, and my last glimpse of them, as we waved to each other,

DEPARTURE FROM JAPAN

was as they moved slowly up the stairs dragging their heavy suitcases. There was no one to help them with their luggage. I had not seen anything of them, except for a few minutes during the last few days, for nearly eight months. Now that they had gone I felt an unbearable loneliness. I walked out of the station with a lump in my throat and tears welling up in my eyes, and then went back to my house, wondering if my own time would ever come.

There was still no news of a British evacuation. I used to go regularly to the Swiss Legation to enquire, but they were never very hopeful. It appeared that, not having been interned, I had but a slender chance of getting away. The evacuation ship, if it ever materialized, would be primarily for diplomats and their staffs. No one else had the slightest claim to be repatriated, and should there still be room after all the officials had been accommodated, civilians who had been gaoled or interned would naturally be given first place.

In July, the Swiss Legation had definite news that the British were going. My name was not on the list, but I was given to understand that there would be a second ship (it has still not sailed), on which I could be certain of a place. It would probably sail in November or December, and I was advised to obtain permission from the police to go away to the hills for the remainder of the summer. Discouraged, I decided to go to the Foreign Office. I had not been there since refusing the broadcasting offer, and I was not expecting a very warm reception. My heart rose when I discovered, however, that the official in charge of repatriation arrangements was a man that I had at one time known well. We had often dined together in the days before relations between our respective countries began to get strained. He was anxious to do what he could to help me, but unfortunately the selection was not in his hands. The list had already been made out at the British Embassy, and he had no power to add my name to it. He was as friendly as ever, hoped I should stay on in Japan, and was in favour of my going up to the hills. Naturally, I was bitterly disappointed, but at least I knew exactly how matters stood, and I made my arrangements to go away for the rest of the summer, for it was now unbearably hot in Tokyo. I sent in an application to the police and a few days later they telephoned to me. I supposed it was to tell me that my request had been granted, but it was not. Imagine my joy when they said that I was to sail with the diplomats in forty-eight hours' time, and that I must have my luggage ready for inspection by them and the customs officials by nine o'clock the following morning. I was also told that I could take with me only clothing and certain specified household belongings. For some unknown reason it was forbidden to include any

DEPARTURE FROM JAPAN

household silver, and linen was limited to two blankets and a like number of sheets. It was strictly prohibited to take any books out of the country; nor could any manuscripts, letters, written or printed matter of any kind whatsoever be included. The Americans, when they left, had been allowed to take one Bible each, but this indulgence was not extended to me. I never discovered whether this was due to oversight, or to the official view that American citizens were more likely to profit from religious instruction than the perfidious British.

I worked all night, stripped to the waist, for the humidity was almost intolerable, and somehow managed to pack up my more essential belongings. Before going out to Japan I had been told to provide myself with a morning suit and top-hat. These I felt I could leave behind without regret, but I was worried about my address book. I knew I should be lost without it, for it contained the names and addresses not only of all my Japanese friends, but of all those in England and other parts of the world. It was while I was struggling with my packing that it occurred to me that here at last was a use for my despised top-hat. During the night I typed out all the more important names and addresses on a piece of thin toilet paper and had just finished concealing this in the lining of the hat when the police arrived. I suppose it was a foolish thing to do, for its discovery might have led to my detention in Japan, but in the event the hat was not examined.

The customs officials, together with several police inspectors, arrived at my house at about eleven o'clock in the morning, by which time I had somehow or other managed to get ready. But they made me unpack everything. Then they carefully examined each suitcase to see if I had concealed anything in the linings. Next they looked at every article I was proposing to take, examining my clothing piece by piece and checking it against the detailed list which they had ordered me to prepare. I had even been made to specify the exact number of handkerchiefs I was taking out of the country. My cameras and field-glasses, which had been confiscated on the outbreak of war, were handed back to me, and I was allowed to pack them in one of the trunks. After this the customs authorities sealed all my boxes, and the police removed them. I was told that I should find them on the ship when I embarked the following day.

I had been up all night and was feeling almost exhausted, but there was no time to rest, as I had been ordered to be ready at five-thirty the next morning, when a police official would call for me. First, I went to the bank, and not being allowed to take any money out of the country excepting a small travelling allowance, I transferred my balance to the account of a Japanese friend, who had previously intimated his willingness to look after my affairs, should it ever become necessary. This done, I spent the rest of the day hurrying madly round the city and saying good-bye to as many of my Japanese friends as I could run to earth. My house, with the furniture, books, gramophone records, and so on, I did not attempt to dispose of; there was not time. By ten o'clock at night I had done everything that was possible in the way of clearing up my affairs and was just about to retire when a visitor was announced. It was the collector of income-tax, who had apparently just received news of my imminent departure from his local police inspector. It appeared that the tax was claimable for the whole of the financial year which at that date had only run a couple of months. I pointed out that since my earnings in Japan would cease with my departure, it seemed rather unfair to ask me to pay taxes up to April 1943; but it appeared that this was the rule. The situation was such, however, that I was no longer in a position to pay. I had already transferred my banking account, and was only in possession of the small amount of actual cash which the government had allowed me to keep back for the expenses of the journey. The collector saw well enough that this would not, in any case, enable me to meet his demands, but like all his kind he had no idea how to deal with a situation for which no provision was made in his regulations, and so it was nearly midnight before I could induce him to go away. As it was, I had to sign a paper making over my furniture to the income-tax authorities.

The police inspector arrived punctually at five-thirty the following morning, and together we set off to the local police station, from which some sort of prison bus was to take me to the railway station. I had lived in the same small house for nearly four years and had grown very fond of it. I had been lonely at times, especially during the past eight months, but I had spent many pleasant hours in this fragile little building. It seemed all wrong, to be leaving it almost furtively at dawn, and to have to abandon all my books and other treasured possessions. We walked slowly along the street, and I turned for a last look as we came to the corner. My faithful old housekeeper was still standing at the gate, and as I waved for the last time she bowed low in ceremonial fashion.

POSTSCRIPT

I HAVE TRIED TO MAKE A TRUTHFUL SKETCH OF THE JAPANESE PEOPLE IN wartime, and have confined myself almost entirely to describing what I personally experienced and saw. The wider field of Japan's political, industrial and economic life lies quite outside my scope, and yet I feel that I cannot conclude this book without casting a glance into the future. What, I ask myself, is Japan's future going to be?

That the Japanese will suffer defeat I cannot doubt; but I find it quite impossible to picture what shape that defeat will take. And, similarly, of our victory I can forecast nothing, except that it will not be an easy one.

The Japanese army, as the reader knows, now has complete control of the government. The army in fact *is* the government. Every branch of the national life: education, industry, commerce, even religion, all are now subject to its will.

That army is now committed to a plan of almost unlimited aggression. It must conquer or perish; there is no other alternative. And the people will be ready to support it to the end. The Germans cracked in 1918, and there is every reason for supposing that in due course they will crack again. But the psychology of the Japanese people is different, and I believe that they will never give in; they will go on lowering their standard of living, if necessary until the daily ration is barely sufficient to support life, but the people will not crack. It is only by complete physical destruction of their men and their resources that they can be defeated; and until we are in a position to bring this about, any talk of a Japanese collapse is merely a dangerous form of wishful thinking.[1]

This, at any rate, is my view, and in support of it let me quote a few lines from a recently published pamphlet by Mr. Joseph C.

---

[1] Dr. J. T. MacCurdy points out in a recent book (*The Structure of Morale* Cambridge University Press. 1943) that the Japanese character is such as to fulfil the conditions for perfect morale. "Single defeats," he notes, "even those that obviously presage ultimate disaster, should not dishearten this warrior nation. If they surrender it will be for purely tactical reasons and will not swerve them from their purpose. I can see no cure for this cancer in the body of humanity except its extirpation. Perhaps, because we are dealing with psychological and not physiological factors, the 'cancer' will starve itself to death. . . . For the present, however, it would seem that psychological considerations do not justify any hope of a breakdown in Japanese morale, but at least they indicate the possibility of their tactics becoming suicidal."

POSTSCRIPT

Grew, who has had unique opportunities for appraising the situation. Not only had he lived for many years in Germany, but for the ten years immediately preceding the attack on Pearl Harbour he was American Ambassador in Japan.

"Probably no other factor," writes Mr. Grew, "has contributed more heavily to the preliminary victories achieved by the Japanese in this war than the offensive spirit which permeates all of the armed forces of the Empire. This spirit, recognized by competent military men as the most vital intangible factor in achieving victory, has been nourished and perpetuated since the foundation of the modern Japanese Army. The Japanese High Command has counted heavily upon the advantages this would give them over less aggressive enemies. They attach great importance to the former disunity in the United States over the war issue, and they still count on an appreciable interval before an aroused nation can find itself and develop a fighting spirit of its own. By that time, they feel, Japan will be in complete control of all East Asia. When they struck, they made no provision for failure; they left no road open for retreat. They struck with all the force and power at their command. And they will continue to fight in the same manner until they are utterly crushed.

". . . I know my own country even better than I know Japan, and I have not the slightest shadow of doubt of our eventual victory. But I do not wish to see the period of our blood, sweat and tears *indefinitely and unnecessarily prolonged*. That period will be prolonged only if our people fail to realize the truth of what I have just said, that we are up against a powerful fighting machine, a people whose morale cannot and will not be broken by economic hardships, a people who individually and collectively will gladly sacrifice their lives for their Emperor and their nation, and who can be brought to earth only by physical defeat, by being ejected physically from the areas which they have temporarily conquered, or by a progressive attrition of their naval power and merchant marine which will finally result in cutting off their homeland from all connection with and access to those outlying areas—by complete defeat in battle." [1]

To this I have only to add that I believe it to be of the utmost importance for the war to be brought home to the people of Japan themselves. They know so little of what is happening in the world to-day, that only when the war is actually brought to their homeland itself will they realize they are beaten. Nothing less than an occupation of the country will be necessary; not necessarily a very

[1] *Report from Tokyo.* Joseph C. Grew. Hammond, Hammond & Co., Ltd. London, April 1943.

POSTSCRIPT

long one, but one long enough to make the fact of *our* victory and *their* defeat incontestable.

During the period of occupation the demilitarization should be commenced, and it is essential that it should continue until the war-making power of Japan is destroyed. Only when this demilitarization is assured should Japan be given a place beside the peaceful and democratic nations of the world. This, then, should be the programme: Defeat, Occupation, Demilitarization, Opportunity.

The period of occupation should be made to depend upon the ability of the Japanese to produce a new form of government; a government with liberal ideas that is willing and anxious to co-operate with the Allied Nations. I believe that the nucleus of such a government already exists in Japan. The country has always possessed liberal-minded statesmen in sufficient quantity. But these men, at the present time, dare not voice their feelings; to do so would be to invite assassination, or, at the very least, imprisonment and torture.

The chief task of the army of occupation would be to ensure that the new government is afforded protection and help while it is reorganizing the administration of the country.

It will be important not to lose sight of the danger lest an occupation be continued for too long, and thus bring odium upon the new government. It might well be found that the presence of foreign troops was making it harder and harder for the government to carry on. Nothing should be done to incur the grave risk of sowing the seeds for a war of revenge. It should be remembered that secret societies have always played a large part in Japanese political life. A great many of these have military backing, and many of their officials are retired military men. Every soldier is more or less forced to join one of them after he leaves the service, and after this war a very high proportion of the adult population of Japan will consist of soldiers who have lost their occupation. It is certain that the activities of these so-called "Patriotic Societies" will tremendously increase.

A great deal will depend upon the position of the Emperor. While it is true that he has always been held in great veneration by the people, his present almost divine status is of comparatively recent invention. This myth has been built up gradually by the army for its own ends. The Naval and Military leaders have always had direct access to the Emperor; it has been in their power to have all important decisions promulgated in his name by Imperial Rescripts. Those decisions are thus protected from all criticism, for an Imperial Rescript is looked upon as holy; it cannot even be criticized, let alone disobeyed.

POSTSCRIPT

Any attempt to discredit the Emperor would, in my opinion, be disastrous. What we must do is convince the Japanese people that their Emperor has been led astray by his military advisers. If this could be successfully accomplished it would have the effect of discrediting the army, and would thus strengthen the position of the new government. The whole-hearted co-operation of the Emperor would be indispensable.

To sum up, the goal of all our efforts will be to bring into being a peace-loving and contented Japan, an agreeable partner in international politics, a country that will contribute to a single, unified world-economy. So, if we intend to demilitarize Japan and control her key imports, as it would seem we must, we shall have to find an outlet for her economic energies. We must be careful not to injure the foundations of Japan's economic life; our task is to show her how to build a better structure upon them.

A peace-loving and contented Japan, however, will only come into being when the government is able to satisfy the needs of the people; that is to say provide them with plenty of work and food. And this surely is an international as well as a national problem. It calls for the creation of the sort of world in which a defeated Japan *can* return to sanity. And the future world-order will be largely determined by the kind of government we have in England and the United States. If, for instance, America decides to return to isolationism, or if we in England choose as our rulers the kind of person who thinks of, say, Czecho-Slovakia as a far-off country with which we have no concern, then the whole world will again be plunged into chaos.

It is clear, to begin with, that China, at any rate, cannot afford to be isolationist. She will have to work hard, and will need the co-operation of other countries in the gigantic task of building herself up anew. A great deal will depend upon the future relations of the Chinese and Japanese peoples. The amount of technical and material assistance which the Western nations are able to give to China must always be limited to some extent by the great distances that lie between them. But Japan is close to China, not only geographically, but culturally. In the course of centuries Japan has evolved a culture of her own, but it should not be forgotten that this has its roots in the ancient Chinese civilization. In the past, China has suffered much from disunity, and this has been the chief stumbling block to progress. Conditions have now changed; so much so that the united and progressive China of to-day bears little resemblance to the China of so short a time as ten years ago. But the Chinese have still a long way to go before they reach a standard of technical and

POSTSCRIPT

industrial efficiency which is comparable with the Japanese. It is in these matters that a right-minded Japan can be of the greatest assistance in solving the Far Eastern problem.

The Japanese have always tried to excuse their aggressions on the plea that *Lebensraum* was needed for an ever-increasing population. But if the case they make is plausible, it is nothing more. It is almost certain that after the war this question will again be brought forward, so it will be worth our while briefly to examine the flaws in the argument.

The area of Japan proper is approximately 147,610 square miles. Then we must take into account the island of Formosa (acquired in 1895), Korea (annexed in 1910), and Karafuto (the southern half of Sakhalin island, separated from the Russian Maritime Province of Siberia by the Mamiya Straits). All these together added another 113,000 square miles to the Japanese Empire. The area of Manchuria (which is a Japanese possession in all but name) is 504,592 square miles, more than three times the size of Japan itself. To sum up: in the short space of forty years the territory of Japan has been expanded fivefold. (I have made no mention of the various mandated islands in the Southern Pacific, which passed into Japanese control at the end of the last war. These, although of great strategic value, are of no importance as fields for emigration.)

In spite of this enormous territorial expansion, the Japanese still persist in claiming that there is nowhere for them to go. In actual fact, however, Manchuria, which is capable of supporting an immense population, remains largely empty; and it is only by forcible means that the government is able even to stabilize the Japanese immigrant population of the country. In spite of the density of population in Japan itself, conditions are not yet so acute as to make emigration preferable. And, in any case, the average Japanese does not like to leave his own country and settle in a foreign land. When he does so, he finds difficulty in adapting himself to changed conditions.

In this brief summing up I have perhaps unduly simplified the question of Japan's surplus population. International agreement after the war must give the Japanese release from economic pressure, otherwise they will go back again to making guns in order to get "butter." This must mean a comparatively liberal policy in tariffs, emigration and so on, in order that the economic life of the Pacific can be established on a more permanent basis than it ever was before. It is not at present possible to foresee what the United Nations will be prepared to do. It does seem, however, that the difficult question of racial equality will have to be settled once and for all.

It is too early yet to speak of territorial settlement after the war,

POSTSCRIPT

since all depends upon the general strategic plan for international security. But obviously Manchuria must be returned to China; and possibly it will be found expedient to grant independence to Korea under some sort of international protection. More than this it would be foolish to prophesy.

I am very conscious of the fact that I have done no more than sketch the vaguest outlines for the post-war treatment of Japan; but I believe that some such policy as I have suggested would make possible the regeneration of the country, provided always that the other Powers were prepared to give full, active and continuous co-operation in the treatment of Pacific problems. All depends upon the good sense and the goodwill of the United Nations after the war.

THE END

London.
November 1942—June 1943.